Rainbow

A Star-Studded Tribute to
Judy Garland

Rainbow

A Star-Studded Tribute to

Judy Garland

edited by *Ethlie Ann Vare*

 BOULEVARD BOOKS *New York*

RAINBOW: A STAR-STUDDED TRIBUTE TO JUDY GARLAND

A Boulevard Book / published by arrangement with
Ethlie Ann Vare

PRINTING HISTORY
Boulevard trade paperback edition / January 1998

All photos reprinted by permission of Globe Photos.

The Putnam Berkley World Wide Web site address is
http://www.berkley.com

ISBN: 1-57297-334-X

BOULEVARD
Boulevard Books are published by The Berkley Publishing Group,
a member of Penguin Putnam Inc.,
200 Madison Avenue, New York, New York 10016.
BOULEVARD and its logo are trademarks belonging to Berkley Publishing Corporation.

PRINTED IN THE UNITED STATES OF AMERICA

10   9   8   7   6   5   4   3   2   1

To Bill Wilson and Bob Smith

Contents

IV *Myth*

V *Memory*

Foreword by Michael Musto

Let's admit it right off the bat: I'm a Judy maniac. Instead of drinking (too much) or indulging in other intoxicating vices, I partake of Judy's greatness. Her music, movies, marriages, mistakes; her grand pronouncements and missed appointments.

It's the most wonderful ride of a hobby—exhilarating yet totally risk-free. As a Judy maniac, you get to enjoy all the highs of her dazzling stagecraft without having to recreate it or even understand how it operated. You get to revel in the nonstop drama of her sometimes misbegotten existence without having to actually *live* the bloody mess. Studying Judy is like watching a continuous soap opera whose characters somehow fall apart and entertain you at the same time. And so I cry with Judy, yell "All aboard!" with Judy, declare "I'm Mrs. Norman Main" with Judy, and roll around in all of her glorious excesses—up to a point. You see, unlike Judy herself, I *do* know when to quit. I have limits. I have perspective. And when the mania becomes a bit too frenzied, I pull back for survival's sake and think about Barry Manilow instead.

Judy's genius shines brighter than ever, reducing all that tragic-lady mumbo jumbo to a historical footnote that becomes invisible once you press "Play." The genius validates our need to endlessly dissect and appreciate this performing powerhouse, and since Judy would have turned seventy-five this past year, it's as good a time as any to take the dissecting and appreciation to a level of manic fervor. By now, I've developed my own little study of Judyism to the point where I've divided her career into three significant stages. Okay, I'll tell you. First, as the tremulous girl pouring her heart out to Mr. Gable or dreaming of a more peaceful place where bluebirds fly, Judy captivated us with the pure honesty and idealism of adolescence. This fleshy young thing had already tapped her way around the block a few hundred times, but she managed to make us believe she was caught in the throes of new, exciting emotions. Judy made these sprightly ingenues eloquent in their adorable greenness—and when she teamed up with Mickey Rooney, all of MGM took on a weird sort of teenage glow.

And then, growing up in front of millions, Judy tackled screen personas that began to mirror her new adult stature. In a host of sometimes surprising, sometimes forgettable musicals, she emerged as a surefire singing/dancing/acting threat who could still make us shiver with a quiver, but mostly delivered us a strong leading lady in total command of her many talents. Even Lassie wasn't as self-assured.

And there was one more incarnation to come (we're talking Judy, Judy, Judy). It was in her twilight years, when personal problems seemed to have an inexorable effect on her work, that Judy shone most brilliantly of all, her pain rising to the surface and grabbing the microphone with the vengeance of a true diva. The tremor became a wail, the misty-eyed ingenuousness turned into smoky anguish, and as Judy sang the hell out of "The Man That Got Away," it became clear that those adolescent dreams hadn't quite worked out as planned. In fact, the boy next door had turned out to be a big, smelly creep. And then Judy went and lost the Oscar to Grace Kelly too!

After her nonetheless triumphant *A Star Is Born* performance, Judy became even more of a bellwether of hurt (though I'm still counting this as part of the third Judy persona—the tragic chanteuse—okay?). I don't think I'm alone in feeling that her most riveting incarnation was on *The Judy Garland Show*; the bizarre variety series almost always seemed to present a star verging on some kind of physical or emotional collapse. Not only was there the constant dramatic subtext—will she make it to the end of the song? Is she even *doing* the same song as the band?—but Judy was clearly teetering on some scary precipice brought out the dark majesty of her talent as well. We sat on the edge watching her on the edge. Veering on caricature, she took breathtaking chances with her material, going so far beyond pop singer clichés she couldn't even be considered in the same business as those "Hey, where ya from?" types. Even a pleasing ditty like "Have Yourself a Merry Little Christmas" took on deep, heartbreaking overtones as she imbued it with a sort of frail desperation. And when it seemed as if Judy couldn't possibly give any more, she didn't (though Liza was craftily waiting in the wings, as if but one more trick to keep the Judy show going).

This compilation of essays, assembled by my fellow cultural scribe Ethlie Ann Vare, deconstructs Judy on every level, from young to not-young, from movies to records, from giving to self-aggrandizing, and as a camp, a cult, a troublemaker, and a superstar. I most admire her as a supreme all-around talent who matched the extent of her range with a rapacious eagerness to explore it. Never has anyone seemed more alive in front of an audience, living to entertain, thanking the crowd endlessly for indulging her indulgence, offering to sing them all and stay all night—for starters. You got the feeling that after the last encore she might wither away and disappear, so, like a kid applauding the fairies in *Peter Pan* to life, you clapped and screamed and begged her to do just a dozen more. Nurtured by our enthusiasm, she obliged, making *I Could Go on Singing* into a life-long motto.

An old-style gay icon for her trembly vulnerability (today's gay movement favors stronger, more unapologetic models such as Madonna), Judy appealed to anyone who ever tore his or her hair out pining for a loved one. It's too facile to just focus on the weepy Judy—this book certainly doesn't—especially when some of her most remarkable moments had her getting a kick out of other people's pain for a change. But we do keep coming back to Judy-on-the-brink because this almost mythic character makes us feel lucky that *we're* not former MGM child stars and even luckier to be constantly able to grab a peek at her dark power. Yes, I'm Michael Musto, and I'm a Judy maniac.

—Michael Musto
New York City, 1996

Acknowledgments

I thank the people who made this book possible because, as we all know, completing a book is essentially impossible.

The ideas flow from an unstoppable creative geyser named Elizabeth Beier, my editor. They are grounded by my worldly wise agent, Madeleine Morel. They are made concrete by my fabulous research assistant, Kimberly Ball.

These people insist that I do have a part in here somewhere, but I'm unconvinced.

This project was aided and abetted by the hunters and gatherers at the Margaret Herrick Library in Beverly Hills, the Warner Bros. Collection in Burbank, the UCLA Research Library, and the seemingly unlimited resources of the Los Angeles Public Library. Support your local libraries, folks—they support you.

I also thank the legions of Garlandophiles who made the quest so enjoyable: my cyberpal, Rick McKay; diarist Johnny Meyer; Garland collector Michael Benson; and my *Gossip Show* cohort, Michael Musto.

I thank you for picking up this book and, most especially, I thank Judy Garland for being so magically, charmingly, frustratingly, and, finally, tragically larger than life.

Introduction

This is the third book in the *Legends* series, a collection of patchwork-quilt biographies that track the life and work of America's great cultural icons in the words of journalists, critics, commentators, and fans. It's pop history as we saw it, before we knew it was history. The series started with *Legend: Frank Sinatra and the American Dream* and went on to include *Diva: Barbra Streisand and the Making of a Superstar.*

But nobody is more perfectly suited to this style of you-are-there, do-it-yourself biography than Judy Garland. Her life was written in the headlines. She grew up in public; she was as we saw her. Judy Garland is a textbook study in the gap between perception and reality.

She was on stage at the age of three. She was on screen at thirteen. Her first duet, her first date, and her first diet were all fodder for fan magazines. She was a child of the studio system, the star system. These guys didn't just use spin control on public information; they invented it. Back in the happy-face, naive 1930s and 1940s, stars didn't have drinking problems and drug problems and sex problems. They sipped champagne from the occasional slipper. The only sexuality was hetero, and even then always within the confines of marriage. It was up to us to read between the lines.

With our 20/20 hindsight, we know now that Judy Garland was the poster child for dysfunctional living. Booze and pills and tempestuous marriages in quantities that today's Brat Pack couldn't even compete with. But which trip to the hospital for "exhaustion" was a drug overdose, and which a suicide attempt? What does "nervous breakdown" mean in Judy's world? Even as late as 1964, the headline in the *Los Angeles Times* read "Judy Garland Treated for 'Injuries to Wrist.' " At least they put it in quotation marks.

The writers of that headline, and the rest of these stories, weren't stupid. Some of the smartest journalists in the world are in this book. But they were playing by the accepted rules of the day. On top of that, Judy herself lived in a denial so far reaching that she apparently stopped differentiating truth from reality before she hit thirty. She actually said on the set of her short-lived TV show in 1963, "I never in my life have had too much to drink, when I work or when I don't work. I really don't drink that much." This from a woman hospitalized with a liver distended from here to Pittsburgh.

This book isn't about the dark side of the Judy Garland story, though. The meticulous, if salacious, *Judy Garland: Secret Life of an American Legend* by David Shipman turns over all those rocks. *Heartbreaker* by Johnny Meyer is pretty heartbreaking, too. This collection isn't about whether or not Judy's dad and second husband were gay, or whether she herself had lesbian lovers. This book is about the public Judy, the Judy we saw on stage and screen, heard on record, watched on TV. This is about the teenaged belter from *Babes in Arms,* the small-town girl of *Meet Me in St. Louis,* the tragic survivor of *A Star Is Born.* This is the Judy that wowed them at the Palace and the Palladium—and doesn't every town have a Palace or a Palladium? This is the Judy whose voice could bring you to tears because her pain is your pain—even if you had no idea what her pain really was.

I am always touched by the irony of the exchange between Judy and Charles Bickford in *A Star Is Born,* when they agonize over her alcoholic husband, played by James Mason. Demands Judy, "What is it? What makes him want to destroy himself?" "Don't you think I've tried through the years to know why, to help him? I don't know what the answer is," Bickford cries. "You don't know what it's like, to watch somebody you love crumble away bit by bit, day by day in front of your eyes, and stand there helpless," says Judy—or is screenwriter Moss Hart co-opting the words of anyone who cared about Judy herself? "Love isn't enough. I thought it was. But love isn't enough for him." No, it never is. There's never enough adulation, never enough applause.

In another day, another time, Judy Garland would have been thrown into the Betty Ford Center and given the chance to shake her demons. Hell, she might be alive today at seventy-five, chugging coffee in some AA meeting somewhere, telling bawdy stories of old Hollywood to the newcomers. It's a nice image. But then, it would probably have ruined her delivery of "The Man That Got Away."

This volume collects some remarkable commentators and observers, to create a multilayered picture of the complex star. We have a conversation between Judy herself and the Tony/Oscar/Drama Critics Circle Award–winning author/playwright/composer Noel Coward; it's a gas. There's also an unlikely conversation between Judy and Pulitzer Prize–winning political humorist Art Buchwald.

Before he wrote *Marathon Man, The Princess Bride,* and *Magic and Heat,* before he won those Oscars for *Butch Cassidy and the Sundance Kid* and *All the President's Men*, William Goldman wrote about Judy Garland in *Esquire* magazine. Before Shana Alexander came into our living rooms as a commentator on *60 Minutes*, she wrote about Judy in *Life*.

We have opinions about Judy's work from Ralph Gleason, cofounder of *Rolling Stone* magazine and one of the most respected jazz critics in history, alongside the thoughts of Bosley Crowther, the esteemed drama critic from the *New York Times*, and noted film historian Richard Dyer. Those doyennes of American popular journalism, Adela Rogers St. Johns and Hedda Hopper, both weigh in with their points of view. Essayist Barbara Grizzuti Harrison adds a touching footnote with an in-depth interview of Liza Minnelli.

On a more personal note, performance artist Rick McKay and acerbic *Village Voice* columnist Michael Musto speak to what Judy Garland has meant in their lives.

Bits and pieces, dots and splotches—all in the words of pop culture's most incisive chroniclers. Think of it as a pointillist painting of ideas. Stand back from the canvas and get a colored, nuanced portrait of the icon known as Judy Garland—the mythic life of an American legend.

I Magic

Let's Get Personal: Revealing Intimate and Intriguing Details About Judy Garland

Judy has what she calls "insane" food habits. She likes to eat corn on the cob with grape jelly. (She once dropped an ear of corn in some grape jelly by accident and it tasted swell.) She never eats any two things together. If she has meat and potato on her plate, she eats all the meat first, then all the potato. She never eats on time. If dinner is at seven, she stalls around until eight. She loves to eat hamburgers (but *not* with onions!), little thin hot cakes and wienies just before she goes to bed. She says they make her sleep like a log.

When she drives herself in her little red coupé, she has only one window open and all the doors locked. She sings with the radio as she drives. She likes to listen to the radio only when it is on as loud as possible. She has a portable radio in her room at home and two others in other parts of the house. She usually has all three of them going at once, at the top of their etheric lungs. She likes to feel that the orchestra is right in the room with her. She and Mickey have this bond in common: they both like noise and plenty of it. Her mother and sister are contemplating the addition of a sound-proof room to the house for the sake of their ear-drums.

She's always going to the movies, goes at least three or four times a week. She likes double features; she wishes they would have "treble" features. She likes to sit in the fifth or sixth row from the front, eat candy, chew gum and put her feet up on the back of the chair in front of her. And she

sees her favorite pictures over and over again. She saw Bette Davis in *Dangerous* fourteen times. She saw Bob Montgomery and Maureen O'Sullivan in *Hideout* six times. She has already seen *Rebecca* three times. She cries horribly in pictures when they are sad. She says, "I cry right out loud." The only time she ever really laughs is when she sees a comedy film. Otherwise, surprisingly enough, she doesn't laugh often. When she is pleased or amused her whole face brightens, but she doesn't laugh aloud.

She bites her fingernails and stuffs money in her pocketbooks and sweater pockets and forgets she has it. Once a week she goes through all her pocketbooks and pockets and finds "a little fortune I didn't know I had." She steals combs. She doesn't mean to, she just absent-mindedly picks them up at hairdressers and from her friends' dressing-tables and makes off with them. She has a good memory for telephone numbers and addresses but a bad memory for names. She starts to introduce her best friend to someone and can't remember her friend's name.

Judy has lived in Hollywood, in Beverly Hills rather, for five years. She has had only one contract, a seven-year one with Metro-Goldwyn-Mayer, and still has more than two years to go on it.

Judy loves to go "basement" shopping. She always feels so good, she says, when she finds a bargain. Her favorite dress last summer was a little cotton dress she found for $5.95. She wore it steadily for weeks. She always buys too many things, she says, things she doesn't really need. Especially sweaters and skirts and shoes. More especially, shoes. She has a ridiculous number of shoes, seventy-three pairs at the last count. She has to buy her own shoes for pictures, "which accounts for the jillions I own." She is always planning to give some of them away and then, at the last minute, changes her mind. She has a terrible time parting with anything old even if she can't use it. Her dream is to have a home with a roomy, old-fashioned attic where she can store away the accumulation of her lifetime so that her great-grandchildren can find the things in the years to come. She is, she says, "a natural-born 'saver.'"

She loves to go shopping at the Five & Ten. Her bureau drawers are cluttered with little jars of hand lotions, little boxes of powder and little packets of soap. She loves to shop in drugstores. In the "ritzy" drugstores she just "nose-shops," she says. That is, she goes around sniffing and sampling all the expensive perfumes. She gets hay fever from some kinds of perfume. From Arpege, for instance, which is her favorite. Paul Whiteman gave her four bottles of imported perfume when he worked with her in *Strike Up the Band* and she went around sneezing for six weeks. "Better to sneeze than not to smell like *that*," she explained.

Judy loves the "corner" drugstores, too, like the one in Hollywood where Cliff Edwards takes over the cash-register when the girl is off and Bob Taylor comes in and whips himself up a malted milk and everyone drops in and "dishes the dirt." She'd like to live in a small town and hash things over the back fence.

She is five feet two and a half inches tall, weighs one hundred and eight pounds and grew just exactly an inch in this past year.

The singing Garland has never taken but one singing lesson in her life and that was in New York a year or so ago. She sings from her chest. The "toney teacher" to whom she was recommended had her bring her voice up in her throat by inserting a pencil in her mouth. The result was that Judy couldn't talk and the teacher criticized her "poor diction." She also made her practice singing while blowing on pieces of paper! Judy got out of that *atelier* in an hour and a half and never went back.

She hasn't any superstitions but she has quite a bevy of pet phobias. She can't climb a ladder, for instance, she falls right off. If she stands on a chair, she falls, too. She has an "in-back-of-me" phobia. When she is driving she always feels that someone is about to crash into the back of her car. Head-on collisions never trouble her, it's that in-back-of-me bogey. Sometimes, at home, when she's the last to go to bed, she remembers that she forgot to turn off the downstairs lights. She goes down to check. And feels sure that someone is in back of her. She tries to keep herself under control by saying, "There is no one in back of me, there is no one in back of me," but all the time she is walking faster and faster until, like Dorothy in *The Wizard of Oz*, she looks as though she is being carried along by a hurricane until she is whisked into her room and the door banged shut. She also had a phobia about bumblebees or anything, except snakes (she *likes* snakes), that crawls or flies. She gets hysterical when a bumblebee buzzes in her hearing. Spiders are her downfall. When she finds a spider in her room she calls her mother, her sister *and* the help to rout the invader. She doesn't mind mice. She rather likes them. They have such cute ears, she says, and "look so hopeful."

Judy hates to wear hats, except little "college" hats, the kind you wear on the back of your head, or turbans. She has a mean hand with turbans; she can swing them as no-one else can, her girl friends say. They're always asking her to wrap theirs for them. She's a very sympathetic girl, her friends also say. When they have any troubles or problems, they always take them to Judy. She always manages to straighten them out.

Her watches never keep time. They're always slow. Perhaps they've given up trying to keep up with Judy, who always goes fast. She never walks anywhere, always runs and usually the hop, skip and jump kind of a run. She has seven watches—gifts from different people—including a lapel watch, a finger-ring watch and a key watch. The key watch is a tiny watch inserted into her house-key and was given her by the sponsors of the Harvest Moon Ball. When it's five-thirty in the afternoon her watches always say it's two-thirty—all seven of them. She never worries about anything. She thinks worrying is "so futile." She says she always does the very best she can and, if that isn't good enough, she forgets it.

Judy dreams almost every night. Always the same kind of a dream. She dreams that she wakes up and talks to somebody or calls someone on the phone. And then, when she does wake up, she can't be sure whether she really dreamed it or not and has to call the person to find out. It's very confusing!

When Judy goes on dates she doesn't like to get all dressed up and go to swanky night clubs, except once a month. She likes to go to other kids' houses or have them come to hers and just roll back the rugs, dance, play records and talk. She never was a violent jitterbug. She jittered some, but not much nor for long. She likes to rumba. The week before she finished in *Strike Up the Band* she had all the kids in the cast, Mickey, June Preisser, Margaret Early, Bill Tracy, Leonard Sues and the others, up to her house. Mickey and about five other kids stayed on after the others left and played badminton and went night-swimming in the pool. Judy likes to swim at night because there are no bumblebees in the moonlight. She just acquired a swimming pool this year and now Sunday afternoons have become very "open house" at the Garlands'.

One of her best girl friends is pretty little Betty Jane Graham. Judy's best friends are her old friends, which tells a little tale in one sentence. Judy and Betty Jane first met when they were six years old and both tried out for a part in a Universal picture which starred Slim Summerville. Each young-ster thought the other would get the part so they didn't like each other. They were rivals in rompers. Neither of them got it (Cora Sue Collins did), and Judy and Betty Jane have been pals ever since. Betty often comes to the studio with Judy, sits with her while she has her hair done, her make-up put on, and stays with her on the set. Every hour or so, the girls send out for chocolate malted milks or cokes. Leonard Sues is another grade school pal of Judy's and Betty's. The three are inseparable. Leonard plays the trumpet in the band in *Strike Up the Band.*

Judy writes poetry. And loves to read it. She has written ten poems of her own—ten, that is, that she hasn't torn up. She is her own severest critic and if she doesn't like the poem, she destroys it. She has done an oil painting, too—a landscape.

She always reads the funny papers and buys comic magazines by the bale. Her favorite movie actors are Clark Gable and Cary Grant. Cary is on the M-G-M lot now, working with Katy Hepburn in *The Philadelphia Story.* Judy sees him in the commissary every day at lunch-time. He always says "Hulloa, Judy," and she answers, "Hulloa, Mr. Grant." Judy is frank and friendly, but there is none of this "Hi, toots," calling people she doesn't know well by their first names. She wears a pleasing mantle of dignity over her friendliness, and it is very becoming. Her favorite movie actresses are Bette Davis and Margaret Sullavan. Her favorite stage actress is Katharine Cornell. She has never met any one of them. She would like to be "of the school" of Davis and Sullavan. She is not, she says, "depending upon her singing." She is delighted because in her next picture, *Little Nellie Kelly,* she plays her own mother. It's the first time she's played a character part. She is taking it very seriously as, some day, she hopes to be taken. She trails around after her mother, copying mannerisms and "making notes."

On the set of *The Wizard of Oz,* Director Victor Fleming always called her "Ange." She doesn't know why. Busby Berkeley, directing *Strike Up the Band,* calls her "Butch" and calls Mickey "Stinky." Mickey always calls her "Jutes" and her mother and sisters call her "Judaline."

When Judy and Mickey are working together, the set is a three-ring circus, with one round of crazy acts after another going on. Judy helps Mickey with the songs he writes, making suggestions and recording them for him. She has a record-machine in her dressing room. Louis B. Mayer gave it to her on her last, her eighteenth, birthday.

Her favorite radio programs are the New York Symphonic Concerts. She always listens to them on Sundays. If she is up late enough (she goes to bed at nine o'clock when she is not dating), she always listens to the *Rhapsody in Wax* broadcasts. She also likes *Information, Please* and the *Lux Theatre of the Air.* She has two favorite types of books, biographies of musicians and memoirs of doctors. Judy used to want to be a doctor or a designer. Now she's decided to "concentrate on my own career." She loves pets but likes to have only one at a time. She has a little, blonde cocker spaniel. She doesn't care particularly for cats because "they're never friendly." And she doesn't like birds for pets "because you can't pat them." She likes pets you can cuddle. Her favorite song is "Over the Rainbow." She *does* sing in the shower.

Judy has what she calls "happy unforgettable things" and "unhappy unforgettable things." A "happy unforgettable" happened when she made her personal appearance tour in New York three and a half years ago. For the first time, she saw her name in electric lights on Broadway, that dearest dream of all true troupers. An "unhappy unforgettable" is when the studio made her give up her new motor bike. It was a Christmas gift. It had a rumble seat among its many attractions. Into the rumble Betty Jane would hop and off they would go. One day they meant to drive into a Drive-In but somehow, they not only drove into it but *over* it, counters and all!

Judy's biggest athletic thrill of the year was when she and Bill Stoefen played Paulette Goddard and Bill Tilden on the Ambassador courts and each side won a set!

Her room at home is very tailored. The color scheme is beige, chartreuse and dark brown. Jackie Cooper's mother, who has gone into the interior decorating business, did Judy's room. The chairs and divan are upholstered in a soft, dark brown suede. The drapes are chartreuse, unruffled, severe. There is a fireplace in the room and it *works*—overtime. There are no frills nor cushions nor little "hobby shelves" around and about. Judy doesn't collect anything but books and records. The only visible trinkets on her dressing-table are some graduated saddle-boots holding perfume. One side of the wall is devoted to autographed pictures. Gable's, of course, Jackie Cooper's, Freddie Bartholomew's, Robert Stack's, Mickey's also, of course, and Cary Grant's which has recently been added. The others are pictures of non-professionals. Now Judy is planning to "go feminine." She wants to do over her dressing-room, "like something Marie Antoinette would have whipped up." She's going to have thousands of yards of chiffon drapes and mirrored walls and do-dads and gew-gaws.

A little girl in a Santa Ana hospital could tell you how warm Judy's heart is. The little girl was dangerously ill and in her delirium she talked constantly about Dorothy in *The Wizard of Oz*. The child's mother wrote Judy a little note and told her about it and asked Judy if she would be kind enough to send the child an autographed picture of herself as Dorothy. She thought that when, or if, the fever broke, it might help her little girl through the crisis if she could find a picture of Dorothy where she could see it. Judy did better than that. She took the autographed picture to the hospital herself. And when the little girl came out of the fever, there was the living Dorothy standing by her bed. The doctors say there is no doubt but that the child's recovery, certainly the rapidity of her recovery, is due in substantial part to Judy.

Unlike most screen youngsters, unlike most youngsters, perhaps, Judy has a horror of "going glamorous." "In the first place," she says, "I'm not the type. For one reason or another, glamour just doesn't appeal to me. I'd rather bicycle across the country, or go on picnics, or play handball on the beach than any other things I can think of. And glamour girls aren't supposed to do things like that." As a matter of fact, Judy is so afraid that some day, albeit unconsciously, she may "hit the glamour trail" that all of her friends have been warned by her to be on the watch for any sign and, if any should appear, to squelch it before it gets a healthy start.

Judy graduated from the University High School in Sawtelle, last June. She wanted to graduate from a real school, not just from the studio schoolroom, so that she could have a real graduation . . . She had one, and there were no photographers present. Judy had no more flowers than the other girls. And she got as many autographs in her Year Book as she gave. She wanted to be "just one of the class" that day, and she was. She had it. Now she is taking a post-graduate course in French.

Judy slipped out of the "sock stage" gracefully and quietly, making the transition so effortlessly that no one has been conscious of it. She looks younger than eighteen and acts younger than the average, sophisticated eighteen of today. She doesn't smoke. She doesn't drink. She almost always wears sweaters and skirts. She uses lipstick for street wear but no rouge, mascara, nor eyeshadow. When she's making a picture she reddens her hair a little for the sake of the camera. She photographs better that way. When she's not working, she doesn't do anything about her hair. She never goes to beauty parlors. She can't seem to "set a date." Whenever she does, some of the kids drop by and say, "Let's have a coke" and what is a girl to do? She says she knows she should diet but doesn't.

Her studio dressing-room is done in navy blue, red and white. It's nautical, with anchors and ship lamps and things. She loves boats and the sea, but as she has never been on a boat for any length of time she says her dressing-room is the next best thing.

For the first time in her life, Judy is learning to read music and having a horrible time with it. She recently bought herself an enormous yellow sapphire ring set with tiny baguette diamonds. It's her first real extravagance, and when she asked the price, it so staggered her that she is buying "on time."

For the last five shooting days of *Strike Up the Band*, Mickey was wearing a class-pin of Judy's.

MGM Press Release

She's grown some from the toddling tot of those days into a star of screen and radio. She's almost five feet three inches tall, but has the same curly brown-red hair, the same big, round brown eyes, and even the same half dozen freckles marching across her nose. She isn't interested enough in make-up to do anything about covering them up. In fact she refuses to use anything but lipstick—no false eyelashes or thick powder base for Judy. She washes her own hair, in fact washes it in the shower and sets it herself. Speaking of showers, she prefers them to the tub—in fact, she refuses to take a bath, does so only when she has a cold and feels that a hot bath before going to bed might help. Then she'll take a bath instead of a shower, slip into pajamas (doesn't like night-gowns), sucks a lemon in bed, and says she knows that she wakes up in the morning minus a cold. Never does she go to bed before she takes her setting-up exercises. Worries about being fat but consoles herself that it is only "baby" fat and that she's bound to be thin the older she gets. So she keeps right on eating chocolate cake, ice cream with fudge sauce, spaghetti and chili. She hates salads, but loves candy bars. When she has ice cream for dessert she'll forego a candy bar, but when she has cake she has candy too. However, she always says she's dieting. Perhaps it's because she remembers the time orders were issued the waitress in the studio commissary to give Judy soup no matter what she ordered. It didn't matter where Judy sat, or what she thought she was going to get—it was always soup. But she only weighs 110, so she doesn't worry.

She's as enthusiastic about her pet likes as she is about her friends. When she buys one dress she thinks particularly lovely, she buys it in all colors—but likes blue best. And she hates to throw away old clothes. Has her closets stacked with them. Once a year cleans out and gives them to the Good Will, but it is like parting with old friends. However, everyone is welcome to borrow her clothes. Shares them with her sisters and friends—but not her shoes, which are her favorites. Has them in all colors—size 5B. She likes sport clothes best, and can't resist costume jewelry, has three bureau drawers filled with "gadgets." She takes care of her own clothes and own suite of rooms, although Fleming and Leona, the two household servants, enjoy waiting on their young mistress—but that's taboo in the Garland home. When she feels sorry for herself over some fancied slight, she plays sad music and cries to herself. Then plays her favorite game of "Pretend" and envisions herself a great opera singer, or a glamorous beauty, or a brilliant lawyer. After she feels sorry enough for herself, she finds her woes have disappeared. She loves to attend sad movies where she can cry to her heart's content, but then is embarrassed when she comes out with red eyes and nose.

In fact she admits being sentimental. Doesn't want to grow up hard and sophisticated. She clings to her little girl habits. Still says her prayers at the foot of her bed and the last thing that meets her eye before turning out the light are two portraits—one of her mother and one of her dad.

She has beaus, is developing into a beauty—celebrated her eighteenth birthday with a real grown-up party at Ciro's—has scores of friends, but still clings to her old ones—is thrilled with her new brothers, Bill and Jack, 19 and 21, and her new sister Ruth, her own age. They are the Gilmores, and Judy's stepbrothers and stepsister, since her mother's marriage last year to William Gilmore of Santa Paula. She has as much fun at the Gilmore home in Santa Paula where she is just little Judy, and where Bill and Jack are the celebrities because they are stars on California's football team, as she does at glittering Hollywood premieres. It's fun to hero worship once in a while instead of being hero-worshiped. She's growing up in other things too. Biographies, travel tales, literature of art and music are replacing her favorite "girl" books. Music is a thrilling adventure into the masters rather than a series of swing tunes for jitterbug steps. She realizes the great influence her mother has had in her life. Knows the courage, patience, and tact it took to manage and keep happy the three little girls, particularly after her dad's death. She hopes to catch her mother's character on paper some day—so that others will know her strength.

But she also admits to still thinking the "Call of the Wild" the greatest motion picture, and can't help a weakness for cartoons, especially Madame Cluck, the Barnyard Opera Singer. She isn't afraid of anything except thunderstorms, is an expert driver, believes she has the "cutest" dog in Hollywood even though he is a giant St. Bernard named "Sergei" who knocks you down by just wagging his tail.

Judy Garland—star at eighteen—is still young enough to be impatient for the future—yet old enough to think it's fun to remember.

Groceries and the Gumms

In some places, the audience thought our act was so bad they threw things at us. Everything. I'll never forget the time someone hit poor Susie in the stomach with a piece of cheese. We didn't have enough sense to pick it up and save it. We could have used it. We were like the Cherry Sisters, only not quite as bad. They had to work with a net in front of them, to keep from getting killed by all the stuff that was thrown at them from the audience. People used to gather food to go in and see the actors.

—Judy Garland, 1964

MGM Production Notes: "The Wizard of Oz"

THE "WIZARD" COMES TO LIFE

CHAPTER 1

A WOMAN IN A GRAY HOUSE

In a gray frame house only a block from Hollywood's busiest corner, lives the widow of L. Frank Baum, a man whose mastery of fantasy has captured the hearts of children and adults for forty years.

It was in this house that the author of the famous "The Wizard of Oz" wrote many of his beloved stories from 1911 until his death in 1919. He and Mrs. Baum built the house in 1911, selecting the site because it was close to a sleepy little country hamlet called Hollywood. Here he could write amid quietness.

Yet today, that home is surrounded by great apartments, a block away walk hundreds of the most famous people in the world, and all about is hustle and bustle.

Although it was not to be until thirty-nine years after he wrote "The Wizard of Oz" that the movies were to capture the charm and appeal of it, Baum was a pioneer in Hollywood. He saw the city only as a quiet place to live, not realizing that one day his famous "Wizard" would be given one of the most costly and painstaking productions in the history of a great industry which was only an infant when he first saw it.

Mrs. Baum will tell you, her husband was always a man with a dream, writing for the joy of writing. He never realized that "The Wizard of Oz" would be the most popular book of its kind in modern fiction, that it would start a whole series of books, and that nine million copies of "The Wizard of Oz" alone would be sold.

"The book, 'The Wizard of Oz,' was only a creation as a sideline to his writing," his widow explains. Baum wrote hundreds of other books, novels, short stories and plays. "Frank read fantasy as a boy and was amazed that so many of such stories were filled with horror and even bloodshed. He vowed that if he ever was able, he'd write a fantasy without such elements.

"He also had a theory that people who remain young are those who never forget their childhood, so he knew adults would love 'The Wizard.' He never wrote down to a child in his life. That is why adults see things in the Oz books juveniles don't. He wove his philosophy into his books and grown-ups saw it and children felt it."

Baum and the illustrator, William W. Denslow, had to publish "The Wizard of Oz" themselves, as no publishers at the time were convinced it would be popular. They said it was too unlike other fantasy books. Within a year after the book came out, publishers clamored for future rights to it.

Baum wrote "The Wizard of Oz" in 1900. It was not until four years later, 1904, that the second Oz book came out, "The Land of Oz." It was thousands of letters pouring into Baum's home weekly from parents and children pleading with him to continue Oz stories that prompted him to write more. Hospitals even wrote that Oz was a part of the treatment for child patients.

Mrs. Baum recalls how artists and writers visiting their home would insist on dramatizing the characters and events of "The Wizard" for their own amusement. So Baum began work on a musical version of his story. It opened in Chicago in 1902 with Fred Stone and Dave Montgomery as Scarecrow and Tin Woodman. It ran there until 1903 when it went to Broadway and remained there four years. Montgomery and Stone took it on the road for a year and then second companies continued for seven more years.

At the time of his death, Baum had written fifteen Oz books, one being published each year. Those original books still sell at the rate of 100,000 a year with "The Wizard of Oz" always being the leader—it is estimated twenty-five million have read it to date. Since Baum's death, publishers have found it necessary to continue Oz adventures with another writer carrying on Baum's characters. To date, thirty Oz books are on sale in bookstands all over the world.

Mrs. Baum can sit in the same chair her husband once used, his legs hanging over the arms as he wrote Oz stories in long hand, backhand, left-handed. Outside is the palm he planted in 1911. It is towering now. So are the buildings around the house.

Today, the characters he created are picturized in the most ambitious undertaking in screen history. Six months were spent developing the script perfectly, three months were devoted to tests and rehearsals, six months were given over to production, six more months were necessary to after-production sound and music effects and editing, five months were devoted to experimentation alone and five more to developing music. Workers spent eight months on costumes and sets.

A total of 9,200 actors faced the camera in "The Wizard of Oz," 450 worked on the set behind the cameras and 6,275 on all branches of production. Three hundred and forty musicians and singers made background music possible.

More than 165 arts and crafts were represented in the making of the picture including workers never before used on a production. There were glass workers, color mixers, cellophane experts, flower makers, a sky writer, powder and fire men, magicians to invent new tricks, high voltage electrical experts, water tinters, beard dyers, wig makers, men who painted pictures with felt strips, lightning men, animal trainers, prospective artists, strange noise developers, hedge trimmers and dozens of others.

For the picture a total of 3,210 costumes were designed and made, 8,428 separate make-ups were sketched in color and applied to faces, sixty-five fantastic settings built from 1,020 separate units, 212,180 individual sounds were placed in the picture and eighty-four different effects created for the unusual events of Oz.

A half million feet of Technicolor film was exposed to create the picture. A quarter million feet of sound track was made. In some scenes as many as eight different sound tracks had to be blended to make dialogue, music and background sounds realistic. The film totals nearly 100 miles of footage and as many as 350 huge lights were used on a single set, generating enough electricity to light 550 five-room homes with two 60-watt globes in each room.

THE "WIZARD" COMES TO LIFE

CHAPTER 2

THE IDEA BEHIND A PICTURE

At thirty, most men and women look back upon childhood ambition with many a laugh and often a shudder at the juvenile nature of what, at fifteen, seemed a great idea. But when an ambition carries through from fifteen to maturity, then the idea is worth carrying out.

At fifteen, San Francisco newsboy Mervyn LeRoy wanted to put "The Wizard of Oz" on the screen. LeRoy had read "The Wizard of Oz" as a boy and had followed it with other of L. Frank Baum's adventures in Oz. He had seen Montgomery and Stone's musical extravaganza. He was convinced that it would make a hit picture.

His ambition continued as he grew up and finally became a screen actor, writer and director. So, today, his boyhood ambition is coming true. Just as he planned it. It seems more of a dream to him than did Dorothy's when she went to Oz. LeRoy wanted the best in organization behind the production and he got it. He secured Victor Fleming as director; Fleming directed "Test Pilot" and "Captains Courageous" and now is directing "Gone With the Wind." Fleming would give fantasy characters realism, whereas Hollywood had been telling LeRoy for years that "Oz" could be made in no other medium than animated cartoon.

He secured Technicolor for photography and Hal Rosson, one of filmdom's aces, to be cameraman. He and Fleming got Adrian, designer of clothes for Norma Shearer, Myrna Loy, Joan Crawford, Hedy Lamarr and hundreds of others, to design 3,210 costumes for his characters. They had Cedric Gibbons, set designer at M-G-M for a dozen years, to create sixty-five elaborate sets. Jack Dawn, the man who first created realistic make-ups and did "The Good Earth" ones, created and put on 8,428 separate make-ups. Yip Harburg and Harold Arlen, of "Vanities" fame, were secured to write the music and Herbert Stothart, one of Hollywood's outstanding musical conductors, to score the film. They had 6,275 technicians creating effects and put 9,200 players to work in the picture. And they had money to spend on it all.

LeRoy, who has never made a "formula" picture through such successes as "Tugboat Annie," "Little Caesar" and "Anthony Adverse," knew formula would not do for Oz. But reality was necessary. He set out, with director Victor Fleming, to achieve reality.

First, there is the use of color. Dorothy lives on a drab Kansas farm. The opening sequences on the farm are in black and white photography with a drab tone to the film. The moment Dorothy enters the "Land of Oz," Technicolor starts and carries on.

Secondly, Dorothy's visit into her "fantasy" world is not a fairy story but the world of the subconscious mind. During the cyclone, she is struck in the head by a flying window. She has been dreaming of a land "beyond the rainbow" where, as she expresses it, "you don't always get into trouble." So, her subconscious mind takes her to this imaginary—but very real—land.

All the costumes look like fantastic creatures, yet there is similarity to the persons Dorothy really knows.

The adventures lead the characters in search of what they desire, Dorothy now wanting to get home more than anything on earth. The Scarecrow finds he really has brains because he has figured the quartet out of many a hole. But, unlike scholars, he has no diploma to prove it. He gets one. The lion has more courage than all because he has risked his life. But, unlike heroes, he has no medal. The Wizard gives him one. The Tin Woodman learns he has the biggest heart of all because he cannot even kill an insect. But, unlike good-deed doers in this world, he has no testimonial. He gets one.

And the Wizard: why this "greatest of all greats" is really a humbug when he is unmasked.

As for Dorothy, at the end, she looks about her home and says, "Isn't it funny? This is the place I was looking for all the time. And I never knew it. This is the most beautiful place in the whole wide world!"

But, working out all this was only the beginning of one of the hardest jobs Hollywood ever had—bringing "The Wizard of Oz" to life on the screen.

THE "WIZARD" COMES TO LIFE

CHAPTER 3

CREATING THE CHARACTERS OF OZ

Because of engineering and photographic problems never before encountered in motion picture history, "The Wizard of Oz" is requiring more than a year of preparation, production and editing.

The picture is one of creation and not duplication. Ordinarily in a picture, research is a major part of a film's preparation. There was no research to Oz. The time is yesterday, today, tomorrow. The place, outside of a Kansas farm for the beginning and end, is what everyone sees in imagination.

L. Frank Baum's book had drawings. They were mere sketches, outside of the characters. The costumes of the Scarecrow, Cowardly Lion and Tin Woodman were faithfully duplicated as were some of the people in Munchkinland, the Emerald City and the Witch's palace. Otherwise, all peoples and places were "dreamed up."

Preparations began in the summer of 1938, rehearsals and make-up and wardrobe tests started in August and actual work commenced in September. Until March of 1939, the film was before Technicolor cameras. Today, difficult sound, musical and editing work is being done. The latter job is taking as long as the film was in production.

While set designers were creating the sixty-five sets for Oz, Adrian was scanning the thirty Oz books for costume planning, color men were experimenting with effects never before tried and hundreds of workers putting ideas on paper, the characters were a major problem.

Because it was necessary that the characters be recognizable as fan-favored players as well as like the book people, Jack Dawn went to work creating make-ups which would not employ masks which took away the personalities of the performers.

From the first Judy Garland was set as Dorothy. Ever since she sang "Jingle Bells" in a family act at the age of two, Judy has been on stage or screen. By seven, she was a real trouper with her sisters, Suzanne and Virginia. Trained almost from birth by her parents, she is a singing star at fifteen and was ideal as Dorothy.

First character problem with Judy was the hair. First decision was to use a blonde wig, but this was discarded for her natural tresses, since Baum never mentioned his heroine's hair color in "The Wizard of Oz." Her costume was next. Although she wears only one frock throughout the picture, weeks were spent testing dresses to select the one most attractive yet rural in appearance. Once set, the dress had nine duplicates and Judy wore out all of them.

Because of his rubber-legged style of dancing, Ray Bolger was the Scarecrow choice from the beginning. A Broadway star for years and a huge hit in "On Your Toes," he had gradually built up a screen following through dancing roles in such films as "The Great Ziegfeld" and "Sweethearts."

With straw sticking from boots, chest, neck and arms, Bolger's appearance was identical with book illustrations and the costume worn by Fred Stone in playing the role on the stage for six years. His make-up, chosen after weeks of tests, leaves his face recognizable beneath a thin burlap coating. It took two hours every day to give him his Scarecrow face.

The dance he does with Judy required two months of rehearsing to effect the illusion that he has not a single joint or bone in his body. He also perfected a jointless walk.

Jack Haley was selected as the Tin Woodman because, like Bolger, he was a Broadway eccentric singing and dancing star. However, he worked under the greatest handicap in the film. His entire costume from jointed shoes to a funnel hat was made of metal, so cumbersome it was difficult to sit and impossible for him to get up unassisted if he fell down as often as he did. His costume had to be newly electro-plated every two days. His face was not touched, excepting for a metallic make-up which could be polished with a soft cloth the same as shoes are shined.

Selection of Bert Lahr made the trio of Dorothy's friends 100 per cent musical comedy, for like Haley and Bolger he was a Broadway comedy star long before he entered films. Lahr has been in vaudeville and musical comedy since he was sixteen but was a singing comedian, whereas Haley and Bolger were more famed as dancers.

Lahr's choice as the Cowardly Lion was further prompted by the fact that his face strangely had lion characteristics with very little make-up. His costume was made with real lion skins, weighed fifty pounds and took two months to create.

To fill the role of "the greatest humbug in the world," Frank Morgan was chosen. He plays the Wizard, making the quartet of comedians in the picture entirely stage-trained. Morgan, now an established screen and radio star, plays the Wizard role without any make-up excepting for white hair.

However, he does don various beards and whiskers because, in the story, the Wizard poses as doorman, cab driver, guard and various other persons in the Emerald City.

Margaret Hamilton, who scored as the farm woman who tried to force Wallace Beery into marriage in "Stablemates," was chosen as the school-teacher who later becomes the Wicked Witch. Her Witch costume is solid black and her face a brilliant green throughout Oz scenes.

Billie Burke, long a stage and screen star, plays Glinda, the Good Witch, in a beautiful bouffant, spangled dress, with crown and wand. Outside of her, all the principal characters carry over from Dorothy's real-life to her magic-world. The only characters who don't go to Oz are Charley Grapewin as Uncle Henry Gale and Clara Blandick as Aunt Em.

This group of players was the nucleus with which director Fleming started the picture. But, before cameras turned, dozens of other strange characters had to be located as the strange people of Oz.

There were two exhaustive searches—one for a tiny dog and the other for every available midget in the United States.

THE "WIZARD" COMES TO LIFE

CHAPTER 4

THE STRANGE PEOPLE OF OZ

As everyone knows who has read "The Wizard of Oz," the land created by L. Frank Baum was inhabited by thousands of strange people. There were Munchkins and Winkies, winged monkeys, trees which could move their limbs, birds which made sounds no one ever heard before, people who looked like China dolls and others who dressed in green and lived in an Emerald City.

Although it was no easy task to cast and prepare Judy Garland, Ray Bol-ger, Jack Haley, Bert Lahr, Frank Morgan, Billie Burke and Margaret Hamilton for these roles, this task was simple compared to that of creating the minor characters.

However, there was still one major role to fill. It required a search. The role was that of Toto, the little dog Dorothy takes from Kansas to the land of Oz. In fact, Toto prompts the whole story. Because he bites the teacher,

Dorothy wants to go to a land where Toto is safe from harm. Producer Mervyn LeRoy and Director Victor Fleming had several decisions to make. Should the dog talk, should it be a man dressed like a dog, what kind of a dog should Toto be?

Requests for opinions were voiced. Thousands of Oz book lovers wrote in. The consensus of opinion was that Toto should be a real dog, should not talk and should be a terrier. Then began the task of finding a dog which resembled the few sketches in Oz books and which could do scenes alone, make rescues, dance on his hind legs, escape from a basket, bark on a signal—in short a dog capable of playing the most important dog role since Rin Tin Tin was a star. Final choice was a Cairn Terrier named Terry, owned by a dog trainer. Terry delivered.

The picture's second search was even more exhaustive. Every midget in the nation, who would come to Hollywood, had to be found to play the Munchkins. Baum's book had described and partially pictured them as tiny folk, not dwarfs or gnomes. That description was ideal for motion pictures. LeRoy and Fleming wanted little persons, perfect in every respect except size. That narrowed the field.

At least 100 midgets were necessary. That was a job. The studio turned the assignment over to Leo Singer of Singer's Midgets fame. His own twenty-eight served as a nucleus. In two buses, he scoured the nation, returning to Hollywood with midgets four to a seat. In all, he found 120 midgets. A large apartment near the studio was rented for them. There they lived on a community basis, each helping to do housework and cooking. Their lunches were served at the studio. A commissary all their own was equipped since tables and chairs were in the regular cafe were too large for their comfort.

To facilitate work further with them, six men, each more than six feet tall, were hired to lift the tiny people into position on the set since they were too small themselves to climb ordinary equipment.

The Winkies, or guards for the Wicked Witch, were all six-foot men, because their Hussar-like costumes and armor weighed more than 125 pounds.

Months before the picture started, costumes were being designed. Adrian, who for twelve years has been the style leader of Hollywood, made more than 3,000 individual sketches. All were hand-tinted to match Technicolor requirements. Every garment had to be made to order, since nothing for the land of Oz could be found anywhere in stock.

For the 120 Munchkins, every costume was individually designed. Adrian sought for the doll effect because when a girl enters a dream world as Dorothy does in Oz, she imagines some people small like her own dolls. Hence Adrian used felt for them, exaggerated jewelry and thousands of individually made flowers. A full picture of Munchkinland with the midgets in costume looks like a flower garden.

The Winkies all dressed alike. For the people in Emerald City there were groups all dressed alike, all in various shades of green. In all there were 1,000 extras on each of four different Emerald City sets, a total of 4,000 persons here alone.

Adrian feels the fantastic but colorful use of flowers, tassels, appliqué, capes and cloth jewelry for Oz characters will start a new feminine mode of fashion.

Besides the Oz people, the picture has Winged Monkeys whose wings are patterned after those of the South American Condor, largest bird in existence; Jitterbug trees which must dance; apple trees which pick and throw their own fruit; and hundreds of animals such as barnyard fowls and stock, a "horse of another color" which changes color, crows, owls, bats and ravens. The only trained raven in the world, Jim, was used for one sequence.

Several hundred birds, selected for color plumage, were rented from the Los Angeles Zoo. The collection was valued at $15,000 and represented ninety-eight species from four continents.

Thus were the strange people of Oz conceived and brought to realistic life. But, around them were the most elaborate sets and the most amazing effects in screen history.

THE "WIZARD" COMES TO LIFE

CHAPTER 5

THE WONDERFUL LAND OF OZ

Set designers usually re-create with research as a strong ally. For "The Wizard of Oz," everything was creation with no research. Art Director Cedric Gibbons, instead of making settings which resembled something familiar, began planning sets which looked like nothing in existence.

More than sixty-five sets were designed and constructed. Each was made into a model from the blueprints and color schemes planned out long in advance to give the ideal in Technicolor: the Witch's castle, Munchkinland, Emerald City, the Haunted Forest, the Apple Orchard, the Cornfield, the Wizard's palace and throne room, the Lion's Forest, the Jitter Trees, the poppy field, battlements, corridors and more.

Munchkinland contained ninety-two tiny houses, giant flowers, a public square, a bridge over a tiny river, a fountain, market places and streets. The whole set stood ninety feet high and contained every color possible to photograph.

The poppy field where the Wicked Witch causes the four adventurers to be drugged, covered an acre and a half. Forty thousand red poppies were used and twenty men worked a week sticking the two foot wire stems of the flowers in the set.

The Emerald City was the largest interior set and was made of ornate and queer structures and angles, all of it sparkling in an even dozen shades of green. Much of the set was built of glass. The cornfield where Dorothy meets the Scarecrow was four acres in size, with a road of yellow brick dividing it. Ten thousand corn stalks were used.

More remarkable than the elaborate sets were the feats which had to be effected by craftsmen. First, there was the cyclone which carries Dorothy and her house away in her dream. Technicians worked for two months on research creating the cyclone from the first wind which strikes the farm, through scenes in which the cyclone is seen swooping down upon the farmhouse, until the house settles to earth in Munchkinland. Unusual effects show Judy in the house with dozens of structures and persons flying by outside.

The schoolteacher had to ride through the air on her bicycle and gradually turn into a witch on a broomstick. Later, when Dorothy throws water on her, engineers had to figure out a way for her to melt before the eyes of the camera.

In Munchkinland, a huge bubble comes bouncing from the distance, changing color as it arrives, then bursts to let Billie Burke step forth. Later it forms and goes bounding away again. Other intricate problems were building trees which could pick their own apples and throw them, having the witch on broomstick write a smoke message in the sky, causing bees to fly from Jack Haley's mouth, nose and ears, permitting the Witch to pluck a ball of fire from the air and toss it at Ray Bolger, having the Witch appear and disappear in a ball of fire, and dozens of other amazing feats.

The film is said to contain more effects than ever before attempted in a film, while the fact that they are done in Technicolor surprises even the experts of Hollywood.

Naturally, the picture was a property man's nightmare because of the fact he had to assemble stranger items than any prop man in history. Many of the items had to be painstakingly built to order.

The Land of Oz likewise was one of strange sounds, which had to be created. Two hundred thousand separate sound effects were worked out for the picture. For one sequence alone, 15,000 feet of birdcalls were recorded at the Catalina Island bird farm, using the 8,000 rare birds there. For the Haunted Forest, these bird songs were blended with two, four and more calls to give bird calls which do not exist.

A marksman spent three hours shooting a .22 caliber bullet at the blade of an ax with microphones recording the whine of the bullet as it glanced from the blade. These, connected into a continuous sound and amplified, furnished the buzz of the "jitterbug."

To effect the sound within the cyclone, mathematicians used more than four million separate figures and algebraic symbols calculating volume and pitch from pressure, velocity, air density and electrical characteristics of cyclones.

For all of this, M-G-M turned loose the greatest manpower organization in screen history. And while they were solving problems, other groups of men were having their own individual puzzles to unravel in the realm of music and color photography.

THE "WIZARD" COMES TO LIFE

CHAPTER 6

THE GLAMOUR AND TUNES OF OZ

Not only did producer Mervyn LeRoy obtain outstanding experts such as Victor Fleming for direction, Cedric Gibbons for sets, Adrian for costumes and Jack Dawn for make-up but he secured the services of the outstanding musical adviser in the industry, Herbert Stothart. Famed for his scores in "Mutiny on the Bounty," "The Good Earth," "Romeo and Juliet" and Jeanette MacDonald–Nelson Eddy pictures, Stothart set to work creating a 100 per cent musical score for "The Wizard of Oz."

It is the first picture to have music every foot of the film, the music ranging from song and dance numbers of magnitude to faint tremolo effects. Georgie Stoll, orchestra conductor, worked in association with Stothart on the background music.

The numbers were written by E. Y. "Yip" Harburg and Harold Arlen, creator of music and lyrics for "Life Begins at 8:40" (with Bolger and Lahr), "The Show Is On," "Hooray For What," and the Varieties on Broadway.

Because the songs tell portions of the story in catchy lyrics, they will be likened to Gilbert and Sullivan songs, but the two explain they really give Gilbert and Sullivan entertainment value in the popular mode which singers can learn quickly. The songs do not stop plot action, nor are they synthetic. They not only continue the story but enhance the characterization.

Arlen, who wrote the melodies of "Stormy Weather," "Let's Fall in Love" and "Only a Paper Moon" has made every number melodic, especially in a popular song, "Over the Rainbow." Harburg, famed for lyrics to such songs as "Brother, Can You Spare a Dime?" and "April in Paris" treated the lyrics humorously, with a twinkle and with tricky rhymes.

In their songs, they had to consider character, plot, reason and entertainment with the hard task of successfully making lyrics both sophisticated for adults and understandable to children.

Critics who have heard the songs already are commenting on the skill with which they are done. For example, the same tune is used for "If I Only Had a Brain" for Ray Bolger, "If I Only Had a Heart" for Jack Haley and "If I Only Had the Nerve" for Bert Lahr. Yet, by use of words and musical presentation style, they give a "corny" quality to the first, a "brittle" one to the second and a "tear" to the third song.

To put in the musical score, for scenes between the songs, Stothart used orchestras ranging from a symphony group of 120 pieces to select swing and small instrumental groups. Choruses for vocal numbers totaled as many as 300 voices.

It was not only a musical but a colorful world that Dorothy stepped into when she visited Oz. To contrast the difference between her everyday world and her dream one, black and white photography with a special tint was used for the Kansas sequences and full color for everything in Oz. Most of the film is in color.

Color problems and discoveries were many. The strange trick of Oz required weeks of research to do in color. In one sequence Dorothy is in black and white photography looking out of the door upon Munchkinland all in color. Harold Rosson, photographer on "Captains Courageous," "A Yank at Oxford" and dozens of other big pictures, was chief cameraman with a Technicolor staff.

Practically every costume was fancifully colorful and Rosson had to work out a list of "relative color values" that filled six typewritten pages to guide make-up and costumes. Color showed that Judy Garland has dimples, that black and white does not reveal!

Color tests were made before every scene, costumes and make-ups light measured three times a day to make sure color work was perfect. Each evening, cameras were taken to a shop and tested, while color filters were changed, lenses polished and mechanisms adjusted. They were returned by morning, ready for work.

Each morning, the huge sound stages were chilled to 52 degrees. As soon as lights were turned on, temperature rose to 70 degrees where, by pumping in air of 52 degrees, a level was maintained. More light was used on "The Wizard of Oz" than any film in history. On the two dozen largest sets, 250 huge arc lights were used, drawing 30,000 amperes of current, or enough to light 550 five-room homes with two 60-watt globes in each room.

Color men believe "Oz" will point the way to hundreds of new uses for natural tones and reveal effects which will astonish experts who were not in on their creation.

B.O. (Before Oz)

Research was an important item of every picture, but *The Wizard of Oz* disregarded it altogether.

Technicolor and black-and-white photography had never been accomplished in a single scene.

Imaginary and unreal sounds had never been created from real sounds, giving both reality and the nonexistent at the same time.

Magicians had never been employed solely to create camera and mechanical tricks in front of a camera using Technicolor, which could not be tampered with.

No picture had ever been given a 100 per cent musical score every foot of the film.

The world had never been combed for every available midget (no dwarfs) to work in a single motion picture sequence.

Double exposure had never been accomplished on Technicolor film.

Set designers had never purposely tried to create sets that "looked like nothing on earth."

No one had ever tried to imagine how a straw man and a tin man sound when they move, because no one had ever seen such men.

Although generations have mentioned them, no one had ever sought to show "a horse of another color."

Not since Rin Tin Tin was a star had any studio ever ventured to give a little dog a main character role comparable to Toto.

No one had ever hoped to successfully put adult appeal into a fantasy story by use of music, effects, sparkling lyrics, and a philosophy, thereby making fantasy of all-age appeal.

No one had ever tried to make a lion out of a man, make trees dance and speak, make monkeys fly, or photograph a jitterbug if one is a bug.

But, then, no one had ever before tried to film *The Wizard of Oz*. No one had recalled that it has had the greatest sale of books of its kind in modern fiction. No one had even ever dreamed that *The Wizard of Oz* could be filmed.

That's why, today, everything in Hollywood dates B.O.

B.O. means "before Oz."

It also stands for "box office."

Fantasy and Myth

The Wizard purports to teach a disaffected and slightly mutinous girl how to fit in at home, in her community—in the System. And yet while she's in Oz she learns anything but subservience. On the contrary, she defies the power structure when she kills the two witches and virtually deposes the humbug Wizard, liberates the underclass in the persons of the Munchkins and the Winkies, and apparently leaves behind her an enlightened oligarchy to be led by her rehabilitated comrades.

—Ethan Mordden in *The New Yorker,* 1990

Babes in the Woods

They went to school together, Mickey Rooney and Judy Garland.

He was five feet tall, weighed less than 120 pounds soaking wet, a cocky, pugnacious ball of fire, always up to his neck in trouble. He was the most important person in the fourth largest industry in the greatest industrial country in the world.

She was a chunky youngster, the plainest girl on the lot, funny face, all eyes, simple, humble, gentle, merry and shy. No idea how to wear her clothes. She was the next most important person in the top production company in that industry.

Their schoolroom, where they learned the history of the United States and recited irregular French verbs, was in the middle of the glamour and color and excitement and activity of a big studio. But Mickey and Judy looked like any other American teen-agers. When they stood shoulder to shoulder, as they did off the screen as well as on, they represented what in another art would have been called Young Genius, in another business literally billions of dollars in assets.

Pillars of The Movies, no worries about the box office, no empty theatres in the days when Mickey Rooney was Andy Hardy and Judy Garland as Dorothy in *The Wizard of Oz* sang "Over the Rainbow." Yet—they always reminded me of Babes in the Woods.

When problems of life far beyond their years caught up with them,

they clung to each other. Before they were out of school, they'd lived nine ordinary lives, known glory and trouble and challenge such as come to few even in three score and ten. They seemed to me to think that no one could understand them as they understood each other. They were the only two who knew exactly what it was like to be in their spots, so high and mighty and yet so fraught with difficulty. So they fought each other's battles with the studio, comforted each other in puppy romances and never in love with each other, formed a brother-sister alliance that was wonderful to see.

The boy, belligerent, tough, a fighter, defiant and cocksure of himself, loved every minute of it, good and bad, survived, and some day will be greater than ever. You watch and see.

The girl? It almost killed her. Crowds in New York the other day spotted her at her last picture, *Summer Stock,* followed her for blocks; crowds wait outside her hotel. They gather at restaurants she frequents, cheer her on sight, show Judy a love and loyalty which prove the hold she—and The Movies—still have on their hearts. Not in many years have fans shown such a strong public opinion.

Where did they come from? How did they get that way?

Joe Yule, Jr., who later changed his name to Mickey Rooney, joined the act in Albany when he was 10 years old.

Disinterested witnesses, on the same bill with The Yules, insist that Mickey sang snatches of songs at nine months. There can be no question that he stole his first show at 15 months.

The Yules were Vaudeville, playing weeks and split weeks from coast to coast. Nobody could keep Rooney offstage once he could walk and one night Mama Yule left the dressing room door open. Leave any door open a crack and to this day Rooney will be in the middle of the act. He gets paid four or even five figures a week, but he will entertain for nothing at any party, night spot, or even at home for a pal rather than not entertain at all.

In Hollywood they don't say extrovert, they say Rooney.

Sid Gold and Babe Latour were headliners in the midst of a romantic duet when they became aware that the audience had lost interest in them. A roar of laughter drowned out their melody and turning, they beheld Joe Yule, Jr., clad only in his diapers, giving a reasonably good imitation of Gold.

The headliners knew better than to compete. So Sid Gold said, "I suppose you think you can do this act better than I can?" and Mickey said then just as he would say now, "I hope to tell you." Coming to the footlights, he sang a little number entitled "Pal of My Cradle Days," taught him by his father and mother.

From that moment, in the parlance of show business, Rooney was "on." He's never been off since.

Once, I asked Mickey if he remembered wowing 'em when he was 15 months old. He'd come to tell me an idea for a story. Listening to Rooney tell a story is like trying to watch both the Notre Dame line and backfield at the same time. He bounces, stands on chairs, lies on his stomach and moves the furniture. The living room vanishes as he creates light, scenery and cast of characters all by himself.

At the end of a Rooney session, you are exhausted just watching him, but he bounces away fresh as a daisy looking for new audiences.

"Certainly I remember when I was 15 months old," he said. "It was one of the great moments of my life, singing my first song."

"What were the others?" I said.

For ten seconds—undoubtedly a record—Rooney was still. The rugged character of his face showed, a face of crags, juts, deep-set eyes, strong jaw, impudent nose, ruthless determined mouth. "I've had more than my share," he said. "Wonderful—wonderful—magnificent—life is wonderful. I'd put meeting Father Flanagan when we made *Boys' Town* first. Then entertaining troops overseas. The time they told me I was going to do Puck in *A Midsummer Night's Dream*. Then the first time I saw Andy Hardy on the screen and knew how good it was. The dance Judy and I did in *Strike Up the Band—*"

His every great moment, even Judy, has to do with show business.

I said, "I've heard it said that a lot of your Big Moments were girls."

Mickey looked surprised. "Sure," he said, "I was girl crazy at 12. Or maybe it was 11. Ava Gardner will always remain a Big Moment. I'm glad we were married but two dispositions like ours couldn't live in one house. Mine was worse."

While he was in basic training in Alabama, Mickey, who always falls in love at first sight, married a girl named Betty Jane Rase, and went overseas shortly thereafter. He actually traveled 150,000 miles in Europe and played to more than 2,000,000 GIs.

Betty Jane testified in the divorce court that being married to Rooney was a combination of an open-all-night restaurant and Coney Island. Besides race horses, backing shows, lending money, buying presents, income tax and getting suckered on phony business deals by his eternal high opinion of the human race, one of the things that keeps Rooney broke is alimony.

Back in circulation Mickey whirled dizzily from girl to girl—no Adonis, he is a great hit with the gals because he's more entertaining than half a dozen tall, handsome leading men. Then he met and married actress Martha Vickers. With a baby, on a country estate, she has Mickey under control. Well, he's getting older. Celebrated his 25th anniversary in show business recently. He'll be 30 before you know it.

Rooney is under five foot three. The three girls he married, Ava, Betty Jane and Martha are all Beauties. They are also tall. Never bothers Rooney. His diminutive size hasn't given him an inferiority complex. He thinks he can lick Dempsey.

Right now, Mickey Rooney is a major Hollywood problem. Desperately needed at the box office, he's hard to cast. Too old to play boys, too young for the big star character parts, not the type for romantic leads. Hard to handle because he's been top dog so long. I've made few predictions in this history. I'll make one now. Rooney will top the box office again when somebody hits on the right idea for him. Rooney naturally thinks it will be Rooney. He'll never quit. He once made 40 pictures in 13 months. He'll do it again if necessary and one of them will bounce him back and every time he bounces higher.

At 26, with years of stardom behind her, Judy Garland has a great talent and appeal. But disaster has followed disaster in Judy's life in the last years. Her recent emotional crisis, the fact that she was taken out of pictures long prepared for her, among them *Annie Get Your Gun*, her suspension by the studio where she's been their pet since 1935, her visits to sanitariums.

Movie-goers have loved Judy so long.

Ida Koverman, for many years Louis B. Mayer's right arm, first heard the child sing and once told me:

"A funny little fat girl. I thought it ridiculous to talk about her for pictures. Then she sang, 'Zing Went the Strings of My Heart'—and mine did. That's all there was to my 'discovery' of Judy. I asked Mr. Mayer to listen and his heart went zing, too, and he signed her."

She was 12. In three years, she was a star and ever since she's made the strings of our hearts hum. Movie-goers have rallied to her, they want to keep her in their lives, they feel someone has done something to Judy.

The motion picture industry is fighting to keep her, too.

One of the things that brought about this tragedy was Judy's health. Born to be a husky, plump girl, as she grew into her teens and had to keep slim for the camera, she dieted beyond reason at the same time she worked 18 hours a day.

Then, as her health and strength failed and she was too tired to do much about planning fun such as is normal for any hard-working girl her age, came the kind of "friends" who gather about the wounded, prey on those who lose their feet even for a moment, take advantage of any weakness. Judy's mother fought against them. So did her husband, Vincente Minnelli. But hard as they tried, they weren't able to drive away Judy's "friends."

Judy's emotional life had left her hurt, shattered her confidence. She was so great in The Movies, it is hard to realize that in her own life, Judy was a sort of Cinderella who never quite got asked to the ball.

First Date

It was twenty-one-year-old Robert Stack who beaued seventeen-year-old Judy Garland on her first grown-up date. "I was so excited," Judy confessed, "that I started getting ready at four o'clock in the afternoon."

Bob was supposed to call for her at eight; but nine o'clock came and went with still no sign of him. Judy was fit to be tied when the telephone finally rang. It was Bob, saying he couldn't find her house in the winding streets of Stone Canyon.

"The number is right out in front," Judy started to say, when she remembered that the house had been newly painted and the number had not been replaced.

"I decided not to take any more chances. We had a loudspeaker system in the house, so I hung it out the window and began broadcasting, 'Judy Garland lives here! This is the house where Judy Garland lives!' "

—Kay Proctor in *Movie Mirror,* 1940

Warner Bros. Press Release

Judy's life story began in Grand Rapids, Minnesota, where she was born to Frank and Ethel Gumm on June 10. She was their third daughter. Her parents had met in a motion picture theater where Ethel was a pianist and Frank a vocalist who led the community sings, an important between-shows feature of movie houses of that day.

Even at the early age of three, little Judy knew she wanted to be an actress. Her debut came unexpectedly and with childish impetuousness. It happened on the stage of the Grand Rapids Theater, owned by her father. Her older sisters Virginia and Suzanne had just finished singing "Jingle Bells." Her mother was playing piano for the sisters and her father was busy in the box office.

With no one to grab her, Judy marched herself on to the stage as her sisters walked off, and launched into a solo of "Jingle Bells."

Soon after, the Gumms left Grand Rapids for California, playing one night stands in vaudeville on the way. Judy had become part of the act with her sisters, the girls having separate billing from their parents. When Mother and Dad were on stage, the girls sat in the audience and applauded. When the sisters were on stage, their parents took the turn at applauding.

The Gumms settled in Lancaster, a small desert community 80 miles north of Los Angeles. Judy's two sisters were enrolled in public school and

Frank Gumm took over management of a theater. The family settled down to a normal, everyday life.

But the time hung heavy on small Judy's hands. She began giving impromptu shows for the other kids in the town and finally her parents enrolled her in a child's drama school. She proved an apt pupil and soon became a member of the Meglin Kiddies. The youthful troupe was booked into a Los Angeles theater and Judy, dressed as Cupid, was to sing "I Can't Give You Anything But Love, Baby."

Judy showed up with her left eye nearly closed because of a sty, but she sang anyway. Gus Edwards, famed producer of juvenile acts, came backstage to congratulate the youngster and urged the three Gumm girls to continue as a trio. Edwards' encouragement went a long way and "The Gumm Sisters" again became an established act, in demand for benefit performances at little or no pay.

Finally a real offer from Chicago, guaranteeing a good salary and their name in lights, sent the sisters away from their Lancaster home. Arriving at the Oriental Theater for the opening, the trio saw their name on the marquee—"The Glum Sisters." The sisters were saddened by this unfortunate error, but it brought them a friend, George Jessel, who was on the same bill.

Trying to comfort the forlorn kids, Jessel took Judy on his knee, mopped her tears, and told her she was pretty as a "garland of flowers." Then he stopped—Garland was the name of a well-known New York critic, Robert Garland.

"How about changing your name to Garland?" he suggested. That night "The Garland Sisters" came into being. A year later, Hoagy Carmichael's song, "Judy," inspired the rest of the name. Now the change was official. Frances Gumm was professionally Judy Garland.

After a brief engagement at the Chicago World's Fair, and a run-in with a gangster who wouldn't pay the girls for their performance in his concession, the three sisters and their mother were broke and very hungry. Too proud to wire Dad Gumm, who had disapproved of the Chicago trip, they eventually got a job that earned their fare back to very welcome California.

More schooling and then Virginia and Suzanne—"Jimmie" and "Sue"— met nice boys and got married. Judy's interest turned to school, and she was on the baseball, volleyball and basketball teams and she made many friends.

While on a vacation at Lake Tahoe with her mother, Judy sang for a campfire group. Lew Brown, of the songwriting team of De Sylva, Brown and Henderson, heard her entertain and suggested to Mrs. Gumm that Judy should approach the film studios in Hollywood for a job.

That was all the inducement mother and daughter needed and soon they were making the studio rounds. But at 12 years of age, Judy was too young for adult assignments and too old for child parts. Judy's break came after she appeared at the Wilshire-Ebell Theater on a special vaudeville program. The way this long-legged gangly kid "belted" out a song with sentiment and power won long and continued applause from the semi-professional audience. Within a few weeks she had been signed to an M-G-M contract.

Judy studied in the studio school with Mickey Rooney, who is still one of her close friends, and Deanna Durbin and soon played her first film role in a short, "Every Sunday Afternoon." Then she played in a feature, "Pigskin Parade," on loanout. Judy developed a girlhood crush for Clark Gable, whom she had never met, and with her vocal coach, Roger Edens, composed a song to him. Later the trembling Judy had a chance to sing it to him on a sound stage on his birthday.

The rest is screen and music counter history. The song, "Dear Mr. Gable," introduced by her in "Broadway Melody of 1938" became a great hit. And Judy won fame and a charm bracelet from her dream man inscribed to "Judy, my favorite actress, Sincerely, Clark Gable." Judy is still one of the world's biggest selling record artists.

She won the friendship of other M-G-M stars, who took her to their hearts, and in her next picture, "Thoroughbreds Don't Cry," she was taught how to sing a torch song by the great Sophie Tucker. Later came roles in "Everybody Sing," "Love Finds Andy Hardy," "Andy Hardy Meets a Debutante" and "Strike Up the Band."

Judy was then cast as Dorothy in "The Wizard of Oz," which proved her luckiest picture. It won her an Academy award, presented by Mickey Rooney, the honor of putting her footprints in the forecourt of Graumann's Chinese Theater, and her own home—a sprawling white frame house, with trees, flowers, tennis court and charm-size swimming pool.

Other hit pictures followed—"Babes in Arms," "Little Nellie Kelly," "Ziegfeld Girl," "Life Begins for Andy Hardy," "Babes on Broadway," "For Me and My Gal," "Presenting Lily Mars" and "Girl Crazy." Then she began doing grown-up roles in "Thousands Cheer," "Ziegfeld Follies" and in "Meet Me in St. Louis."

In "The Clock" she proved her ability in a straight dramatic part. Then came the musicals "The Harvey Girls," "Till the Clouds Roll By," "The Pirate," "Easter Parade," "Words and Music," "In the Good Old Summertime," and finally "Summer Stock."

Judy married director Vincente Minnelli on June 15, 1945. Their daughter, Liza May, was born March 12, 1946, and made her screen debut as Judy's daughter in "In the Good Old Summertime." The Minnellis were divorced in March, 1951, with Judy obtaining legal custody of Liza.

The following year she married Sid Luft, a producer, and the couple now have a daughter, Lorna, born November 26, 1952. They recently bought an estate in Holmby Hills.

Judy was one of the first Hollywood stars to tour Army camps and entertain enlisted men in World War II. She was singing for troops at Fort Ord, California, when word came of the attack on Pearl Harbor.

She is very sentimental and enjoys watching sad movies when she can weep to her heart's content. If she buys a dress she likes especially well, she'll have it copied in a variety of colors and fabrics. She prefers sport clothes, loves radio mysteries and soap operas, and admits to a weakness for antique jewelry. She always knows exactly what she wants.

Vital Statistics

Born: Grand Rapids, Minnesota	When: June 10
Eyes: Brown	Hair: Red-brown
Height: 5' 1¾"	Weight: 110

Hedda Hopper

FROM *WOMAN'S HOME COMPANION*   SEPTEMBER 1954

No More Tears for Judy

Hasn't everyone heard Judy Garland sing "Over the Rainbow"? It's become her song, a poignant ballad about a place where dreams come true—a happy land where there is no sorrow.

Judy is making a comeback in pictures. Her pictures always were smash hits; *A Star Is Born* will be too. But a hit can't help Judy unless she comes to some kind of peace with herself. Are her years of tragedy over?

Four years ago Judy was a sick, tired girl with a too-thin face and over-bright eyes. Everyone feared her career was finished. Metro-Goldwyn-Mayer had released her after 13 years and more than 30 highly successful pictures. At that time Hollywood was hard hit and she had cost her studio large sums of money by not showing up for work or by arriving late. Joe Pasternak, one of her producers, said of her then, "Delay with Judy is something she can't help. It isn't that she doesn't care. She has said to me, 'Why am I like this? I don't want to be. I want to work.'"

I remember when Judy was first teamed with Mickey Rooney. I was under contract to the studio at the time and all of us would flock to the set of their picture whenever we had an hour or so off. They were perpetual motion, like high school kids at a jam session. They captured the imaginations of all the other workers at the studio.

Judy didn't happen to be a quick study at dancing then. Mickey was like greased lightning but Judy's thoughts and actions were slower. They were yelling at her all the time. "Come on, Judy. Get the lead out! Move!" She was being driven at top speed—dancing, singing, improvising, building entertainment. She burned up energy every minute of the day. If you've ever watched pictures being made, you know it's not the cinch it's cracked up to be. Especially musicals.

I'd hear Judy say again and again, "I'm so tired. And I'm so hungry." The director would yell, "Come on—get in there! Do this routine again and you'll forget you're hungry."

She was hungry. She had always had a ravenous appetite. Before the studio decided to make a star of her, she devoured wheatcakes, ham, eggs, toast and jelly for breakfast. She loved to top off lunch with chocolate cake and ice cream. Then she was warned she'd have to slim down. Instructions were sent to the Metro commissary that no matter what she ordered, she was to get only chicken soup and cottage cheese.

When you don't eat and you work hard, you get tired. Judy got so tired she was ready to drop in her tracks and took Benzedrine to pick her up. At night, her nerves frayed, she couldn't relax, couldn't sleep. She started depending on sleeping pills.

It began way back there—her long battle with weight, diet and nerves. It was a battle that, unless a halt were called, was bound to become unbearable. No halt was called.

Why would anyone want to go through all this?

By this time, of course, Judy was determined to be a star. But I doubt if she could tell anyone whether she would have chosen to be an actress. She was born of people with the smell of greasepaint in their nostrils. She began performing when she was three.

Her parents, Frank and Ethel Gumm, had toured the vaudeville circuits as Jack and Virginia Lee, sweet southern singers, before their three daughters were born. Judy, born in 1922, was their youngest. Her parents were then living in Grand Rapids, Minnesota, where her father worked as the manager of the New Grand Theater. Even though the father had settled down to a steady job, the mother had not given up vaudeville. She created an act in which the two older girls sang while she played the piano as an added attraction at the New Grand.

When Judy joined the act, the Gumms thought they had something. They began to dream of Hollywood. They worked their way west playing dates as they traveled. But the movie studios didn't want them. Frank

Gumm fell back on his old job as a local theater manager, this time in Lancaster, a small desert town some miles from Hollywood. They lived there nine years.

Ethel didn't give up hope. She groomed her children for show business and they began touring up and down the West Coast. Judy by then was the most ambitious of them all, perhaps because she was the youngest and was trying to show her big sisters what she could do.

Critics panned them. One dubbed Judy "the leather-lunged blues singer." She didn't know what this meant but she sensed that something was wrong and sang louder and louder. They didn't make much money either—one Christmas found mother and daughters eating tortillas at a corner drugstore near the theater they were playing.

They were a hit just once. Ethel had thought they might click at the Chicago World's Fair of 1933 and she got the girls there by playing every town that would take them along the way. By chance, they shared one program with George Jessel at the Oriental Theater in Chicago. The singing trio stopped the show. Jessel was delighted with them—he suggested their names be changed to Garland; he said the trio was "as pretty as a garland of roses." Judy also changed her first name, which had been Frances. Aside from new names, the trio acquired nothing. They had to work their way back to the coast.

The oldest sister, Suzanne, decided she'd had enough of show business and gave it up for marriage. As a last sentimental fling, the trio played The Lodge at Lake Tahoe, California. Here Judy was discovered by Lew Brown, who put her in touch with a Hollywood agent. She was 12.

Judy wasn't much to look at. She was as round as a rain barrel and her hair was stringy. But her enormous hungry eyes had a wistful appeal. And she could sing.

Judy was put under contract at M-G-M. At that same time Metro had signed another young girl—Deanna Durbin. They made a short together called *Every Sunday Afternoon.*

But Deanna got away. Universal was looking for a young girl to play in *Three Smart Girls.* By a fluke Deanna's contract was allowed to lapse at Metro and she went over to Universal. She became a star with *One Hundred Men and a Girl.* She got the royal treatment, put her footprints in the forecourt of the Chinese Theater with those of the theatrical great.

Metro believed that they had lost the greater talent to a rival. They schemed to develop Judy into a counter-star. Judy wasn't reluctant.

A small dramatic role in *Thoroughbreds Don't Cry* gave her the break she needed. The star of the picture was Mickey Rooney, who was becoming the biggest box-office name at Metro with the Andy Hardy series. With the team of Mickey and Judy, M-G-M thought they had an exciting combination. They did—they had a gold mine.

The two youngsters attended the studio school together. They were pals. Naturally Judy had a crush on Mickey but he regarded her as a kid. *The Wizard of Oz* put her on equal footing with him professionally. Then they costarred in *Babes on Broadway*.

At the premiere the kids sat together in the darkened theater. When the lights came on to rounds of applause, Judy was crying. "I know what you're thinking," Mickey said. "We're just two kids from vaudeville and we didn't mean a darn thing. Now it's happened."

The studio sent them to New York for the picture's premiere at the Capitol Theater. There they did six and seven shows a day to capacity business and broke every existing record.

Mickey told me recently that they had only 40 minutes between shows. "One afternoon," he said, "we'd finished our act and gone off stage. We were supposed to come back and take a bow. But Judy collapsed in the wings. I felt something serious had happened to her. She'd been working too hard—going too fast without letting up."

Yes, she had overworked. But now she was sitting on top of the world. At 16, she was a star and owned a home in the exclusive Stone Canyon section of Bel Air. The public idolized her; exhibitors called for more and more.

The pictures were ground out, one after the other. Both the studio and Judy wanted to make them. The studio was getting rich. And Judy couldn't let anyone else take over a picture.

Her old problems of how to work without eating grew worse. Her nerves became raw, insomnia a terror. She couldn't have taken it easy any more if she wanted to; she always had to roll in high gear. She was driven to turning to people who were always on the go. Her friends tried to warn her. Her mother, now a widow, pleaded with her. But it was impossible for her to slow down. She headed for a nervous collapse.

Still the collapse might have been prevented had people accepted her marriage. She'd been in and out of love a dozen times when she met David

Rose, a serious, preoccupied composer some years her senior. They were married on June 28, 1941, when Judy was 19. But from the beginning few of her friends approved of the marriage. I believe she was trying to find happiness in her own way but she didn't have a chance.

So she plunged recklessly on, growing even more popular with pictures like *Presenting Lily Mars, Girl Crazy,* and *Meet Me in St. Louis.* Her career soared and her marriage simply petered out.

She found a new attraction in Vincente Minnelli, who had directed her in *Meet Me in St. Louis* and in *The Clock.* Their wedding took place on June 15, 1945. Vincente was 10 years her senior and had never been married. The studio was all in favor of her marriage. Louis B. Mayer himself gave the bride away. The studio had become worried that she was going too fast and hoped that Vincente would help her settle down.

It was impossible for her to settle down, although none of us really realized it then. She began to have periods of depression when she didn't want to see anyone; otherwise she continued her hectic life. When I learned she was pregnant, I hoped this would change her but motherhood unfortunately doesn't often produce miracles.

The birth of her daughter Liza left Judy in a weakened condition. She recovered enough to go back to work. Glowing reports were issued by Metro as she made such pictures as *The Ziegfeld Follies, Till the Clouds Roll By* and *Words and Music.*

Her ravenous appetite strangely deserted her. She didn't have to struggle any longer to reduce—she stayed thin. She tore through her films on nervous energy and with the help of doctors.

One day I visited her on the set of *The Pirate.* Shaking like a leaf, she took me into her dressing-room and went into a perfect frenzy. She swore that everybody was against her, cried she had no friends.

She went on living recklessly. She and Vincente drifted apart.

Then she was assigned to *The Barkleys of Broadway.*

For the first time she began to fail to show up for work. Production was delayed when she'd refuse to work. She had been a fiend for work for years. Now something desperate was happening inside Judy Garland.

The studio suspended her. She was replaced in the picture by Ginger Rogers. Aghast, Judy begged for another chance. After all, she'd made millions for Metro, she pleaded. They gave her *In the Good Old Summertime* with Van Johnson.

She finished that picture in record time. So Metro bought her the hottest property on Broadway—*Annie Get Your Gun*.

The director assigned to her was a man who had directed her at the beginning of her career. She demanded that he be replaced.

She was given another director. She recorded the songs—collectors' items today that can be had only by stealing them from Metro—and started rehearsals. At this point nearly a million dollars had been spent on the picture. Then Judy didn't show up for work one day.

Metro removed her from the film rather than risk added millions and the possibility of never finishing the picture. Betty Hutton replaced her.

When I confirmed the story and phoned it to my newspapers, I called Judy. Her voice leaped eagerly over the wire. A few days before I had written about the strain she had been under in turning out 30 pictures in 13 years. She was grateful.

"Your sympathy," she said, "gave me a lift just when I needed it badly. I'm leaving right now for a talk with Louis B. Mayer and I think he'll straighten this situation out."

I realized she didn't know she had lost *Annie* and I didn't have the heart to break the news to her. "After you've had your talk with Mr. Mayer, drop by for a chat," I said, knowing she'd need sympathy after that bomb had been dropped in her lap.

Two hours later a tragic little figure walked into my den. There was nothing left of the little girl from over the rainbow. Sad and brooding, she looked as though she'd lived a lifetime in her 25 years.

Everyone knew by now that she wasn't well. In a few days, at Metro's expense, she entered the Peter Bent Brigham Hospital in Boston. But she couldn't stand isolation; she couldn't rest. She got in touch with friends in New York.

When she returned to Hollywood she was 15 pounds overweight. She was given a chance to do *Summer Stock*. She still wasn't well enough to do a picture but she needed the money. And the studio wanted her to do it— by now she was a national institution. People loved her; when I wrote sympathetically of her, I was flooded with letters from grateful fans. One woman wrote that the release of a new Garland picture meant a reunion for her whole family. Small wonder that her race to reduce before starting the picture created inspirational headlines.

She didn't make it before the cameras rolled. If you saw that film, you could almost watch her lose weight. Her first scenes showed her as a healthy plump girl driving a tractor and singing her heart out. The last number revealed a trim-figured Judy in black tights and top hat. Between the tractor and the tights she had lost 20 pounds.

Then Judy began to fail to show up for work; again she was threatened with suspension. She begged for another chance. It was granted and a specialist was flown from Boston to stand by during work on the picture.

Whether Judy showed up for work or not, her costar Gene Kelly was always there. He told Pasternak, "I'll never forget how wonderful she was to me during *For Me and My Girl*. Whatever she does—I'll stick by her."

When Judy did come to the studio, there was always a rose in her dressing-room with a note: "Good morning, Judy." When she was missing for four or five days, the roses—wilted by then—were sent to her house with a note: "We miss you, Judy." Later when she opened at the Palladium in London, there was a fresh rose for each performance with a note: "Hello, Judy." She'll never know unless she reads this that Joe Pasternak, her producer, was the donor.

"I love that girl," he says. "When she was missing, there was something wrong. Delay with Judy is something that is within her. Something that you know she can't help. Everybody at the studio said to me, 'How can you stand these delays? How can you put up with such temperament?' I replied, 'When I look at the rushes, I pray she'll come back *any* day.'"

Somehow Judy finished her strenuous dance routines with Gene Kelly and the picture ended. It was a smash hit. The preview was like an opening night. The audience laughed and applauded every number.

Judy had been promised a long vacation. But she was called back to take over in *Royal Wedding* for June Allyson, who had learned that she was expecting a baby. The studio should have known better but it felt that Judy could do another film if she set her mind to it.

Rehearsals began with Fred Astaire. Then the crash came—with a large cast waiting, she failed to show up one Saturday. The director phoned her home four times only to be told that Judy was on her way. On the fifth call the maid said that Miss Garland wouldn't be at work that day.

Judy was replaced by Jane Powell. Her suspension was announced.

Judy tried to cut her throat. During a business conference with Carleton Alsop (then her agent), Mrs. Jim Tully (her secretary) and Vincente Minnelli, she ran into the bathroom, broke a glass and proceeded to slash her throat. The cut wasn't serious—more a case of pique than anything else—but this attempt should have indicated to everyone how deeply unhappy Judy was, how disturbed.

Judy herself has said, "All I could see ahead was more confusion. I wanted to black out the future as well as the past. I wanted to hurt myself and everyone else."

And as always, she was genuinely sorry for the trouble she had caused. She said that she couldn't seem to help the way she acted but that this wasn't any excuse for her.

We all knew that Judy was through at M-G-M. She had failed to cast in three pictures. She was released from her contract.

Sometime during those next months Judy met Sid Luft. A former test pilot for Douglas Aircraft, he served with the Royal Canadian Air Force during World War II and was married to Lynn Bari, a promising actress. His position has been described as "producer," "theatrical agent," "business adviser." He wasn't one to be pushed around. Perhaps that's why Judy found him fascinating.

Sid Luft suggested that she make a comeback on the legitimate stage. He arranged a tour. First step was London's Palladium.

That appearance was a personal triumph for Judy. She had the English eating out of her hand. On opening night they gave her a three-minute ovation.

From the Palladium she went to the Palace in New York City, the pinnacle of vaudeville. She played the Palace for 19 record-smashing weeks. The theater netted $800,000. Critics wrote about her in superlatives. Her fans were pulling for her, the lonely hearts who seldom, if ever, see over a rainbow in great Manhattan. They all came to her, the loyal ones who had long cried themselves hoarse over their idol and the eager boys who had all but driven her to a nervous breakdown. Romance-starved kids, who lived all her greatness with Judy, closed their eyes to the fact that she was no longer a child but a grown woman.

Roger Edens, the pianist-composer and Judy's old friend, told me that she could have played there a year. But no one could have taken the tough grind of seven night shows and four matinees a week for that long. "She worked an hour and 10 minutes without stopping," he said. "The kid didn't have a chance to breathe until the show was over. The only time she could relax and take a breath was when she paused between bows."

The grind began to tell. Toward the end of the run, Judy cracked. Pains started in her chest. It was believed she had heart trouble. A doctor found nothing wrong with her heart but gave her medicine to relieve the pain. It knocked her out completely.

When she regained consciousness she insisted on going on stage and later described feeling "halfway between the floor and the sky." She forgot her lyrics. Her accompanist, Hugh Martin, desperately threw her the lines. Instinct carried her through to the end. When she was going to stagger back on stage for a bow, she was grabbed and rushed into a waiting ambulance.

To fans who massed at the stage door she said, "Don't worry. I'll be back."

From the Palace she went on a tour of the country which ended in Los Angeles at the Philharmonic Auditorium. Movie stars dread an appearance on their home grounds: they know how critical their peers are. But Judy had a phenomenal opening. Over 2,600 people crammed themselves into the auditorium to greet her. Her opening number was "This Is My Town." From then on the audience was with her all the way.

The Friars Club held a banquet at the Biltmore Bowl proclaiming Judy "Miss Show Business." Everybody in town was invited. Sitting over in a corner was Mickey Rooney. "Everybody was slapping each other on the back," he told me, "and I kept thinking to myself, 'Poor little Judy. How many of these people really care about you?'"

How many really care about an actress as a person is always an unanswerable question. In private life, Judy was now married to Sid Luft and was shortly to give birth to a second daughter. She no longer saw her mother.

Sometimes I think her feelings about her family have to be looked at within the frame of Judy's whole life. Judy herself has said that she always felt as if she weren't wanted. Apparently she felt she had to drive herself, become somebody important, if she expected anyone to want her. Everyone knows that Judy did drive herself. As a little girl of 12 just beginning in pictures, and for years afterward, she did just what was asked of her, even when she was pushed beyond her strength.

But however punitive she seems at times to have behaved toward others, she was much more harmful to herself. After all, by her behavior she brought herself down from Metro's favored star to a girl no studio would take a chance on.

She didn't plan to do any of this. As she has said, "I don't want to act this way. I don't even know why I do."

Like most people, I'm hoping that Judy's years of tragedy and illness are over. Judy seems to believe that they are. She has said that now, for the first time, she has faith in herself, that she isn't a little girl any more but a mature woman in control of herself. We all hope she has realized that whatever the wrongs done her in the past, she did become a star loved by millions.

A Star Is Born will put her back on top. Jack L. Warner helped Judy and her husband finance the film. In these days of economy in Hollywood, the picture has been the talk of the town—it cost $4,000,000. Judy has had ideal working conditions. She didn't have to be on the set until 11:00 A.M.; when she was tired, she just walked off. She can't be suspended: she and her husband are the bosses.

"Judy is very cooperative," one of her co-workers told me. "She has a fabulous enthusiasm for working. She's never lost it."

Insiders tell me she's singing better than ever. As long as she has millions loving her and fighting for her, she can keep her doubts and ghosts buried.

Judy's rainbow looks very bright. Maybe she's found the happy land on the other side where there are no sorrows.

II Mystique

Poem

Would that my throat were blessed by the nightingale
That I could but sing of my heart's great love
In some lonely tree flooded with silver
Sing till I burst my breast with such passion
Sing, then fall dead to lie at your feet

—excerpted from a poem by Judy Garland, age 17

Liza Wilson

FROM *THE AMERICAN WEEKLY*   SEPTEMBER 26, 1954

Judy Garland's Magic Word

Judy Garland and Sid Luft, two young people very much in love, sat close together in their parked car on a promontory of Lookout Mountain. Below them glittered the lights of Hollywood.

"It's beautiful," said Sid, "isn't it?"

"No," said Judy in a strange, frantic voice. "It's ugly. I hate it. I want to get away, Sid. And I don't ever want to come back."

"That's only because you've been badly hurt, honey," said Sid, drawing her closer to him. "You're unhappy and confused. But you're one of the biggest names in show business. You can make thousands of dollars in radio, in theaters . . . you can make millions in—"

"By the way," Judy interrupted, with a tense little giggle. "I'm dreaming of a beautiful steak."

"Sorry, honey," said Sid. "I haven't any money."

"Neither have I," said Judy. "I'm broke."

Almost four years later, Judy Garland had occasion to remember that night on the mountaintop when they had to borrow enough money for a hamburger at a drive-in. It was July 29, 1954, and the last scene of *A Star Is Born* was finished. Cast, crew and Warner Brothers executives gathered around to kiss Judy and slap Sid on the back. As the Lufts left, someone called after them, "You've got a wonderful picture. You'll make millions."

"The last time we were making millions," said Judy with a laugh, "we couldn't even afford a steak. Now we have a beautiful baby, a lovely home and a good picture." Affectionately she brushed her cheek against Sid's coat sleeve. "But I couldn't have made the picture without you, Sid. When I fell in love with you I'd lost all confidence in myself. I was a silly, frightened girl—but your love gave me faith in myself again. Remember opening night at the Palladium in London?"

In the spring of 1951, Judy had borrowed money from her agents to pay for her tickets to London. Sid went with her as her manager. It was her first public appearance since she had become emotionally confused and despondent over her career.

"I was sick with fear, that opening night," she recalls. "Five minutes before curtain time I told Sid I couldn't go on.

"Sid shook me so hard I heard my teeth rattle. 'You silly girl,' he said, 'those people out there love you. You're not going to fall flat on your face.'

"So what do you think I did? I fell flat on my face. I sang three songs. The audience applauded. I started to take a bow. My poor trembling knees buckled—and down I went.

"I managed to get off stage and had no intention of going back—ever. But Sid made me and the audience was warm and friendly."

After the Palladium came the Palace in New York. Sid was still busy bolstering up her ego. But a member of the Palace management, who shall be known as Mr. X, was just as busy breaking it down. He wouldn't paint her dressing room or hire extra ushers. ("Gotta save money. You won't be here long. Won't be many people coming to see you.") But when he refused her a timpani (kettle drum) for the orchestra, it broke what little spirit she had left. One of the musicians said he'd be glad to lend her a timpani.

"No," said Mr. X. "We haven't room in the orchestra for a timpani. We'd have to take out three $4.80 seats—and they are all sold for opening night. We'll need every cent we can make. I don't expect this show to last long."

Came 2:30 in the morning—the morning of the opening. Judy had finished a rehearsal, a rather sad, dispirited rehearsal. She and Sid lingered on the bare stage after everyone else had gone.

"Sid," said Judy, "I just can't do the *Get Happy* number without a timpani. I'll be a flop."

Sid patted her hand. And then, across the stage, he saw a box of tools a carpenter had left.

"Shall we?" said Sid, pointing to it.

"Let's," said Judy.

They unscrewed three seats from the first row of the orchestra and dumped them backstage. They called the musician who'd offered to lend them the timpani. They took a taxi to his apartment in the Bronx. By 5 that morning, the orchestra had a timpani. Well, that night Judy sang *Get Happy* as it never had been sung before and her opening night at the Palace made theatrical history.

Judy, you'll remember, played the Palace for 19 weeks, a sensational engagement that broke the records of such headliners as Kate Smith, Eddie Cantor and Georgie Jessel. On Sundays she liked to drive in Connecticut with Sid. One Sunday Sid said to her, "I've got a picture in mind for you."

"I've got one, too," said Judy. "What's yours?"

"No," said Sid. "You tell me yours first."

Suddenly she became quite shy.

"For years I'd wanted to do *A Star Is Born,*" says Judy. "When I suggested it to Metro, while I was under contract there, they laughed at me. I was afraid Sid would laugh, too. So for 15 minutes we drove along, each waiting for the other to say first. And suddenly we both shouted simultaneously, '*A Star Is Born*!'"

During the pre-production days of the picture, Judy as star and Sid as producer had many problems. ("Sid had most of them. I was busy being pregnant.") Sid wanted the best, no matter what the cost. George Cukor to direct. Moss Hart to write the script. Harold Arlen and Ira Gershwin to do the music. Irene Sharaff to design certain sets and costumes. Dick Barstow to direct the dancing. The studio—one eye on the cash register—tried to offer substitutes. But Sid got what he wanted.

"Timpani became our rallying cry," says Judy. "To us Timpani means: Nothing is impossible. Often I was depressed and willing to compromise, but Sid would shout 'Timpani' and I'd rally for battle. I'm sure Jack Warner thought we were crazy."

One morning, a few weeks after the picture started, Judy woke with a headache. Her phone rang. It was Sid.

"Judy," he said, "what's the matter? We're waiting for you on the stage!"

"I have a headache," said Judy. "I think I'll stay in bed today."

"Timpani," said Sid, and hung up.

Judy was on the set in an hour. Strange what love, and timpani, can do for a girl.

Bosley Crowther

FROM *THE NEW YORK TIMES*   OCTOBER 17, 1954

The Rebirth of a Star

Judy Garland Shines in a Showy Remake of a Famous Film

There seems to be some resentment of the fact that the new *A Star Is Born,* which has Judy Garland and James Mason in the husband-wife movie star roles, is not an exact carbon-copy—nor even a facsimile—of the Janet Gaynor–Fredric March drama that blazed a fire-trail some seventeen years ago, casting a stark illumination upon the irony of fame in Hollywood. And there also has been some criticism of the fact that it runs for three hours and includes a lot of Miss Garland in a repertory of entertaining songs.

The resentment is easy to fathom, since it comes, in the main, from those who have placed their memories of the old film in a sort of emotional shrine and tend them on odd occasions with bouquets of dogmatic praise. This is both legal and decent. *A Star Is Born* was a brilliant, moving film, and those who desire to recollect it with rampant reverence have our entire sympathy. The only thing is, they need not fling their coats off and start dancing with their fists in front of them simply because the Warner Brothers have remade it in a somewhat different form.

The criticism of its length and musical content is something else again, and that we would like to consider on this autumnal Sabbath morn.

Up and Down

What was the situation in the original *A Star Is Born* and what could have been done to improve it by remaking it in a contemporary film? The situation was simply that a drunken, arrogant, famous male film star met up with a little nobody—a hopeful but inexperienced girl—whom he whimsically boomed for movie stardom, fell in love with and wed. And while she was rocketing upward, he was rocketing down, a victim of his own wild self-indulgence and the vagaries of fame in films. In the end, to complete the hopeless fracture that the reversal in their professional prestige had brought to their home, he walked off into the ocean. It was a poignant and ironic film.

Now, it might have been possible and practical to remake this sentiment-loaded tale in a straight organization of dramatic content as one that happened in 1954. It might have bristled with the satire of Hollywood that was in the original, and it might have been made a pointed comment on the irony of the lives of those who manufacture romance, laughs and tears.

But there are two plain and plausible reasons why that might not have been so good. One is that the fashion in straight dramas about the lives of Hollywood people has passed beyond the simple lines of this Nineteen Thirties story. Such stark and corrosive accounts of the natures and behavior of film people as we got in *Sunset Boulevard* and *The Bad and the Beautiful* have set a pattern for the searching and cynical approach. And the other reason is that this story is a bit on the old-hat side. There are not many characters on the cut of this story's hero in Hollywood today.

Therefore, it seems to us quite reasonable that the Warners should have chosen to do *A Star Is Born* as the big sentimental show with music that the remade version is. And it strikes us as artful and rational that such a talented star-within-a-star as Miss Garland is in this picture would show how fully and well she's able to perform.

Legend

To be sure, Moss Hart's re-written version of the drama of the original is neither quite modern or logical as it tells substantially the same tale of the star-crossed love of two people who are beaten by the goldfish lives they lead. But it is rooted in the lore of Hollywood legends, so it is acceptable when the gush of its romance and heartbreak is well-channeled through winning performance and wonderful songs.

And the performances and songs are excellent—the performances, that is, of the two stars, who are the exclusive focuses of interest in this film now on the Paramount and Victoria screens. Miss Garland's rich and spirited singing of a nice collection of Harold Arlen songs is matched by her versatile performance of an undisguised sentimental role. You can believe she has merited stardom from the demonstrations of talent she gives. This is something that few pictures about sensational artists can call upon them to do. And Mr. Mason's performance of the actor-husband is a sharply nettled and flexible one, revealing a tormented ego if not a clearly understandable man.

As for the length and size of the picture, in gigantic Cinemascope, they are appropriate to the abundance of pictorial detail and show-off it contains. George Cukor, with the colorful consultation of Hoyningen-Huene, has composed some brilliant stuff of Hollywood environment and some interestingly allusive things. It is out of such extravagance as one sees here that stars and sensations are born.

Judy's Oscar

As I lay there in bed, in came a flock of TV technicians. I was told that I would have to talk back and forth with Bob Hope, who was master of ceremonies at the awards. They strung wires all around the room, put a microphone under the sheets and frightened the poor nurses almost to death by saying "If you pull up the Venetian blinds before they say 'Judy Garland,' we'll kill you." Outside the window, I could see the cameramen on the tower getting ready to focus on me on the bed. We listened to the whole ceremony, the excitement building up. Then Bob announced the winning actress. It was Grace Kelly.

—Judy Garland, 1957

Press Release: The Museum of Modern Art Department of Film

A STAR IS BORN (1954). Produced by Sid Luft for Warner Brothers. Directed by George Cukor. Script by Moss Hart, from an original screenplay by Dorothy Parker, Alan Campbell, and Robert Carson. Music by Harold Arlen. Lyrics by Ira Gershwin.

Cast:

Judy Garland	Esther Blodgett, Vicki Lester
James Mason	Norman Maine
Jack Carson	Matt Libby
Charles Bickford	Oliver
Tommy Noonan	Danny McGuire
Lucy Marlow	Lola Lavery
Amanda Blake	Susan
Irving Bacon	Graves

Courtesy of Warner Bros. Ca. 160 minutes.

A STAR IS BORN has had a somewhat unhappy history. When the shooting of the film was finished, the producers felt that it was short on musical values and added, without Cukor's aid or approval, the "Born in a Trunk" routine. The film was already long and with the new sequence, it became very long indeed. After its initial release, Warners decided to cut it. Cukor offered to help, but Warners worked alone, removing the better part of two musical numbers and several scenes which delineated (with great charm) the early stages of Vicki Lester's career and the beginning of her romance with Norman Maine. The cutting is extremely unintelligent.

Still, much of the trouble lay in the original concept of the film. It was a full-length dramatic story into which large production numbers had been added rather at random. It had to be too long. Cukor also gives the actors more than enough latitude to establish, underline and dot the "i's" of every dramatic situation. Moreover, James Mason remembers that "Cukor was improvising elaborate endings, lead ins, lead outs of scenes. I knew this was going to be a very long picture and the length was going to be pure embellishment . . ." (*Focus on Film*, April 1970).

In fact, it really is the embellishment that makes this version of A STAR IS BORN so exciting to watch. It was one of the first films to use the cinemascope screen imaginatively and one of the few American films ever to use color with any style. The plot itself is clichéd, and it shifts the relationships between the two leading characters too far in the favor of the woman, but the dialogue is literate and often witty. Cukor's direction is rampant with eloquent directorial touches. Judy Garland gives a striking performance played as though on raw nerve ends while James Mason, almost playing straight man to her, is even better in a carefully shaded, beautifully modulated, and totally pertinent characterization.

No print of the complete A STAR IS BORN is known to exist.

—Gary Carey

Naomi Wise

SAN FRANCISCO MAGAZINE   SEPTEMBER 1983

Folklore from Hollywood

In the bad old days when movies regarded themselves as mere entertainment (not art), the money men threw their used products in the trash. Gance's *Napoleon* was dismantled; worse yet, half the films made before 1950 landed in the garbage. And, on films that *were* kept, the money men often interfered with the final versions, cutting films like buccaneers, in search of more profit from a shorter product, and dispatching the extra footage to the bottom of the Pacific. I'd probably skip seeing the full eight-hour version of Erich von Stroheim's *Greed,* but I do wish the excised five hours still existed somewhere so that somebody else could see it and tell me about it.

Now that cinema has been elevated to its proper status, restorers are desperately trying to reassemble this heritage. One example: *A Star Is Born.*

Before seeing the restored version, I wondered why *this* film, of all films, had been chosen. Although I like the potatoey sound of "Pocatello, Idaho," and the mental image of its "Princess Theater," the rest of the movie seemed heavy and mawkish, a muddy musical soap opera. In the age-old show biz story, a star rises while her mentor (and husband) falls. They suffer at length. Finally, he does the noble thing. Phooey!

Worse yet, I'm not a fan of Judy Garland, and in some respects, the film is *about* Judy. At the time (1954), she was both up-and-coming heroine

Esther Blodgett and down-and-outing hubby Norman Maine, rolled into one bundle of booze and Benzedrine. Her closeups are sometimes painful—dope gets in your eyes. Her singing is good and effective, but I can't stand her persona. In one scene she looks old and puffy, in the next, svelte and insistently perky; and her conspicuous weight changes seem to prey on sentimentality—a feeling once aptly described as "self-regarding emotion." Poor Judy. Poor womankind.

"Women cannot afford to be sentimental," observes a Godard character in *Breathless*. If Judy weren't worrying about her weight, she might be thinking dangerous, analytical thoughts about her situation as victim and how to change the balance of power. Men seem to love sentimentality in women (and thus love Judy Garland). Women can't afford it, lest they *become* Judy Garland.

My other observation has to do with the fabled charm of James Mason as Norman Maine. Seems like a creep from the start. Anyone marrying him deserves what she gets, and Esther walks into a state of misery with her eyes wide open. That's too much masochism for any single movie, and even "Born in a Trunk" could never buy it off for me.

The newly restored, 70-millimeter version shown at the Oakland Paramount gala (and scheduled for release this fall in 35 millimeter at lesser palaces of cinematic art) nearly does buy it off. With funding and assistance from the Foundation of the Academy of Motion Picture Arts and Sciences, restorer Ron Haver has recovered 19 out of 27 lost minutes. Without these extra minutes, the movie was too long. The restored version is just right—or at least, a lot better.

The film was cut because exhibitors demanded it: The shorter a movie, the more showings per day and the more tickets sold. Not only was George Cukor's original version of *A Star Is Born* three hours long, but it called for an intermission—and exhibitors hadn't yet discovered the huge profit potential of the candy counter. Thus, Harry Warner (of the notorious Warner Bros. Gang) recut the film despite Cukor's objections and without his participation. The result was the leaden musical melodrama that Cukor refused to see.

Cukor was a major director of "women's films" and he rarely indulged in mawkish melodrama. His style was light, fluid and immensely witty. *A Star Is Born* seemed atypical; 30 years later, we learn why. What got lost on the cutting room floor was charm. James Mason's charm. Even Judy's charm. And above all, show biz charm.

In some places, where Haver found no film footage, he reshot production stills in sepia and set them to scraps of soundtrack; these are interspersed (charmingly) with the motion footage. While Norman is on location for a sea epic, Esther goes to work (real footage) at a sleazy fast-food drive-in, then gets a job singing to puppets for an idiotic commercial. Norman returns and (in stills) searches for her; comically, he finds her on a tenement roof, drying her hair. Their courtship is filled out, and we discover that yes, he *is* charming, and she's engaging. The restored footage amount to a justification for their loving.

The unkindest cut of all was the removal of a sound-stage marriage proposal that feels more like the interaction of *real* actors than any other moment in this "backstage musical"—it's the funniest scene in the film, with an irresistible picture of the characters in their native milieu. When Esther later puts on a one-woman parody of "Big Musicals" for Norman (most emphatically including those directed by Judy's ex, Vincente Minnelli—especially *The Pirate*), at long last the scene seems funny, not frantic, and genuinely perky. The proposal scene reveals Esther as a witty woman, not merely a suffering dishrag, and sets the stage for the film's own big musical number, the newly restored "Lose That Long Face." Here we have the very essence of "the show must go on" stoicism: Esther is crying over Norman's boozing and her own ambivalent feelings as she applies her giant clownish freckles—and then she hits the sound stage to belt out another show-stopper about the need for optimism. More than "Born in a Trunk," this number is the essence of show biz, and the long lost center of the movie.

The last half of the movie still descends into mawkishness, but 40 minutes or so of sob story is more bearable when it's a smaller fraction of the whole and when the whole is a whole lot better. Now not only is "Born in a Trunk" thrilling, but "The Man That Got Away" means something other than masochism. Support your local film restorer.

Facts and Figures About A Star Is Born

The most talked-about motion picture of the year, Warner Bros.' Cinemascope and Technicolor presentation of the Judy Garland–James Mason starrer *A Star Is Born* used a cast that numbered more than 1,000 stars, featured players, supporting actors and extras—there were 160 speaking parts written into the script by playwright Moss Hart. . . . Malcolm Bert, famed West Coast architect and art director, designed 106 new sets, including a complete beach house in Malibu. . . . The 6,700 seat Shrine Auditorium was used for the opening and closing sequences of the film and for these scenes more than 600 extras were hired. . . . Judy Garland's six new songs in the movie were written by Harold Arlen and George Gershwin. . . . Five months of shooting time went into the production of the drama-with-music and seven months of planning and rehearsal preceded that. . . . One of the most interesting figures in the new film belongs to newcomer Lucy Marlow whose 36-24-36 measurements make her a distracting sight as she plays her role of a starlet trying to impress studio chief Charles Bickford.

—from a Warner Bros. Press release, 1954

Judy Garland and Gay Men

Judy Garland works in an emotional register of great intensity, which seems to bespeak equally suffering and survival, vulnerability and strength, theatricality and authenticity, passion and irony. In this she belongs to a tradition of women vocalists that includes Billie Holiday, Edith Piaf, Shirley Bassey, Barbra Streisand, Diana Ross (but not, say, Ella Fitzgerald or Peggy Lee), who have all been to varying degrees important in gay male culture.

But Garland's image may be identified the most with the gay male audience.

Judy Garland is camp. Several people have tried to define both what camp is and its relationship to the situation and experience of gay men. It is clearly a defining feature of the male gay subculture; being able to pass for straight has given gays the characteristically camp awareness of surfaces, of the social constructedness of sex roles. Gay men's sense of marginality is turned into an excessive commitment to the marginal (the superficial, the trivial) in culture.

Camp is a characteristically gay way of handling the values, images and products of the dominant culture through irony, exaggeration, trivialisation, theatricalisation and an ambivalent making fun of and out of the serious and respectable.

The object of camp's making fun is often a star like Bette Davis or Shirley Bassey, and Garland can be read like that. She is imitable, her appearance and gestures copiable in drag acts; her later histrionic style can be welcomed as wonderfully over-the-top; her ordinariness in her M-G-M films can be seen as camp, as "failed seriousness."

Anybody can be read as camp (though some lend themselves to it more readily than others), but Garland is far more inward with camp. She is not a star turned into camp, but a star who expresses camp attitudes.

Garland's reputation for being camp (rather than being seen as camp) was reinforced by stories that were published after her death. Her own awareness of the gay connection is made clear. "Gay News" quotes Liza Minnelli quoting her mother—"When I die I have visions of fags singing 'Over the Rainbow' and the flag at Fire Island being flown at half mast.'" One person who wrote to me told me that Garland's "last professional engagement in New York City was when she took money under the table singing in a lesbian bar on East 72nd Street called 'Sisters' in about 1968–69. This $50 per session or so was paid whenever she would 'wander in' and pretend to sing 'impromptu' so she could support her drug habit."

The knife-edge between camp and hurt, a key register of gay culture, is caught when one takes together her intense performance of the scene after Norman's death in *A Star is Born* and her remark quoted by George Cukor, who had expressed amazement that she had reproduced such intensity over two long takes: "Oh, that's nothing. Come over to my house—I do it every afternoon. But I only do it once at home."

For the most part, Garland's campiness might be seen as mildly sabotaging her roles and films. (Those who dislike camp feel that it is in fact deeply destructive in its insistently making fun of everything.) Only *The Pirate* seems to use Garland's campiness in a sustained fashion in its play with sex roles and spectacular illusion, two of the standard pleasures musicals offer. In lines and role, as well as the way Garland plays them, *The Pirate* explores a camp attitude towards life.

Judy Garland's last film, *I Could Go On Singing,* made in England in 1962, is her most gay film. It is clearly aware of the gay audience and is in many ways a summation of the gay way of reading her image: emotionality, gay sensibility, androgyny, camp.

One of the letters I received while researching this chapter tells an interesting story:

"When I was 13 or 14, the whole 3rd form at school voted for what film they would like to see at the end of term. My friend and I liked Garland and wanted to see *The Wizard of Oz.* We were labelled as 'poofs' and laughed at for being childish. *Dr. No* was the film they finally chose. I have found out since that my friend was gay. I find it interesting that two gays, unaware of each other's sexual preferences, remained in solidarity for Garland. Furthermore, we were not conscious of her as a gay person's film star."

This letter suggests that the gay reading of Judy Garland was not just something that gay men picked up as they entered the gay scene; it suggests rather that a person identifying themselves as gay (or probably "different") would intuitively take to Garland as an identification figure.

The gay subculture would develop the most elaborated, the most inward of readings of Garland, would pick up on the nuances and inflections of her image that could be read in a gay way. But the classmates of the letter writer clearly sensed, without probably having any knowledge of the composition of Garland's audience, that there was something about Garland which chimed with their sense of what "poofs" were, a connection between image and social identity that the writer himself made intuitively.

There is nothing arbitrary about the gay reading of Garland. Looking at, listening to Garland may get us inside how gay men have lived their experience and situation, and made sense of them. We feel that sense in the intangible and the ineffable—the warmth of the voice, the wryness of the humor, the edgy vigor of the stance. They mean a lot, because they have made expressive what it is to be gay.

FROM *REDBOOK*   NOVEMBER 1961

A Dialogue:
Noel Coward and Judy Garland

They seem poles apart: America's Judy Garland, who can warm 50,000 hearts singing familiar songs in a huge, open stadium, and England's Noel Coward, who acts, writes and directs his own sophisticated plays and musical comedies. But they are devoted friends, and deep admirers of each other's talent. They are equally outspoken about the theater, the public and life backstage, which they discuss with unusual honesty in the following dialogue tape-recorded in Boston shortly after the opening of Coward's new musical *Sail Away*.

NOEL: Let's just—before we start talking—decide what is interesting about you and me, Judy. I'd say that it's first of all that we're very old friends, so that takes care of itself. What is interesting about us both is (a) you are probably the greatest singer of songs alive, and I . . . well, I'm not so bad myself when I do my comedy numbers, and—let's see, what else?

JUDY: And (b), Noel, is that we both started on the stage at about the same age, didn't we?

NOEL: Yes. How old were you when you started?

JUDY: I was two.

NOEL: Two? Oh, you've beaten me. I was ten. But I was—

JUDY: What were you doing all that time?

NOEL: Oh . . . studying languages! No, I started at the age of ten in the theater, but before that I'd been in ballet school. I started in ballet.

JUDY: You were going to be a dancer?

NOEL: Yes. I was a dancer for quite a while. Fred Astaire designed some dances for me in 1923. I was older than ten then, of course.

JUDY: How marvelous! I didn't know that! Did Fred—

NOEL: I don't think he was very proud of the dances, because I don't think I executed them very well. There was a lot of that cane-whacking tut-tum-ti-ti-tum in them.

JUDY: But, to go back, where did your theater . . . Did you have any background? Was there anyone else in your family at all that was—

NOEL: Theaterly?

JUDY: That's it . . . theaterly.

NOEL: No theater. Navy.

JUDY: No theater? How—

NOEL: We didn't know anything about it. My father's attitude was always one of faint bewilderment. But my mother loved the theater, you see, and she took me to my first play when I was five years old. It was my birth-day treat. Every sixteenth of December I used to be taken to a theater. And then I was given a toy theater for Christmas.

JUDY: By your mother?

NOEL: By my mother. She adored—she loved the theater, you see.

JUDY: Yes. Yes!

NOEL: And I was wildly enthusiastic about it and so that's how it all started. I had a perfectly beautiful boy's voice, so I was sent to the Chapel Royal School, where I trained to be ready for the great moment when I gave an audition for the Chapel Royal Choir, which is a very smart thing to be in. I did Gounod's "There Is a Green Hill Far Away," and I suppose the inherent acting in me headed its ugly rear, because I tore myself to shreds. I made Maria Callas look like an amateur. I did the whole crucifixion bit— with expression. The organist, poor man, fell back in horror. And the Chapel Royal Choir turned me down because I was overdramatic.

JUDY (*laughing*): That's divine!

NOEL: Then Mother was very, very cross and said the man who had turned me down was common and stupid anyway. After that we saw an ad-vertisement in the paper that said they wanted a handsome, talented boy, and Mother looked at me and said, "Well, you're *talented*," and off I went to give an audition. That's how I got on the stage.

JUDY: Divine! But it was different for me. I came in with vaudeville. I . . . You know, it was sort of rotten vaudeville, not good vaudeville. I told you this once before, I think. I came in after the real great days and before television. Really, it was awful vaudeville, you know, so there was nothing very inspiring. But my children are being exposed to all the best.

NOEL: Of theater?

JUDY: Yes. I want them to be exposed to it. I think it's rather stupid to be involved in making movies or whatever, and just leave your children every morning—

NOEL: "Mother's going out now."

JUDY: Yes, and say, "I'm going to work now, but you mustn't know where because I don't want you to be exposed."

NOEL: Well, also the children might adore being exposed. Why not enjoy themselves?

JUDY: So I take them along with me. They have been on movie sets, they have been backstage in the wings. They know what I do when I go to work. Sometimes I think that actresses who say they don't want their children exposed to publicity and don't want their children photographed . . . Well, I have a strange, uncanny feeling that maybe Ma doesn't want any attention taken away from her, you know?

NOEL: You can't have secrets from them. If your mother happens to be an actress, you've got to take it on the jaw and understand that you're the daughter of an actress . . .

JUDY: And you know, it isn't a bad atmosphere. It's fun for our children to go to the theater. And I think that as long as I have a good relationship with them and our home life is a good one, the entertainment world can't possibly hurt them. I don't know whether any of them will become entertainers or not. We'll see. My oldest daughter, Liza, is talented and sort of stuck on the business.

NOEL: I'd love to see Liza.

JUDY: She started to dance when she was five.

NOEL: And you encouraged it?

JUDY: Yes. And she's a brilliant dancer, really. But now she has grown up with the best of—of talents. She has seen you. Her father, who is a very, very talented man, has exposed her to the best of the theater, so she does have taste and she does have a talent. Now she's in summer stock. My other daughter, Lorna—she's eight—is the Gertrude Lawrence of Hyannis Port. She's just impossible, and the most beautiful creature who has ever lived, I think. And she's so shocking and bright and cunning and hep. She's such a great actress that we don't know what we're going to do with her. We really don't. I'm sure she's going to turn into something important. I don't have any idea at all what it will be, but it will be startling and flamboyant and—But I'm taking over the whole darn conversation.

NOEL: No, darling, you should.

JUDY: It's funny how Liza is so much like me, a quietness much of the time, a little sedentary, and Lorna is just the opposite, a mercurial child.

NOEL: When I saw you first, Judy, you were a little girl, although you talk about the vaudeville and all those things . . . But of course, that is the way to learn theater, and not acting school—playing to audiences, however badly.

JUDY: Trial and error. Trial and error.

NOEL: Whenever I see you before an audience now, coming on with the authority of a great star and really taking hold of that audience, I know that every single heartbreak you had when you were a little girl, every number that was taken away, every disappointment, went into making this authority.

JUDY: Exactly. Exactly, and it's all—it sounds like the most Pollyanna thing to say, but it is truly worth it—the heartbreak and the disappointments—when you can walk out and help hundreds of people enjoy themselves. And this is only something you can learn through trial and error.

NOEL: Nobody can teach you . . . no correspondence courses, no theories, no rehearsals in studios.

JUDY: No, you can only learn in front of an audience.

NOEL: And if there are people who cannot withstand these pressures, and if they are destroyed by these pressures, then they are simply no good and are just as well destroyed.

JUDY: Do you really mean that, darling? What do you mean?

NOEL: Well, my dear, the race is to the swift. In our profession the thing that counts is survival. Survival. It's comparatively easy, if you have talent, to be a success. But what is terribly difficult is to hold it, to maintain it over a period of years. You see, nowadays, when everything is promotion and the smallest understudy has a personal manager and an agent rooting for her and a seven-year contract with somebody, they don't take the time to learn their jobs. Then after their first success they run into difficulty—

they have personal problems. And when public performers allow personal problems to interfere with their public performances, they are bores.

JUDY: Yes, and if they're haunted and miserable off stage, they are still bores. Because they are entertainers, and entertainers receive so much approval and love—and for heaven's sake, that's what we're all looking for, approval and love. And they receive it every night and in every way. If they are good, they receive adoration, applause . . .

NOEL: Applause, cheers, flowers.

JUDY: And if they insist on leaving the stage and going—Well, I did this for many years. I was the most awful bore. I went off stage and I'd go into my own little mood and remember all the miserable things and how tragic it was—and it wasn't tragic at all, really. I was just a plain bore. And I think anybody who clings to this tragic pose is a *poseur*—a phony.

NOEL: Self-pity.

JUDY: It's self-pity, and there's nothing more boring than self-pity.

NOEL: And it's a very great temptation—particularly when you're a star and you know that you have an enormous amount of responsibility, you are liable to fall into the trap of self-pity. If somebody doesn't please you or something goes wrong, you fall into the trap—you make a scene, which is quite unnecessary. If you're an ordinary human being working in an office every day, you wouldn't behave like that. No, an entertainer has to watch his legend and see that he stays clear and simple.

JUDY: But you've always done this, Noel. Now, I've known you for years. You've always done this. You are a terribly wise man who in spite of many facets of talent and brilliance and so forth has kept your mind in complete order and your emotions in order. You have great style and great taste. Weren't you ever inclined to fall into a sort of self-pity?

NOEL: Oh, yes, yes, yes.

JUDY: Oh, good. It makes me feel much better, because I really did it for a long time.

NOEL: After all, Judy, darling, I'm much older than you.

JUDY: Not much any more, darling. Nobody is.

NOEL: I've been in the theater fifty-one years, and all my early years were spent in understudying, in touring companies and everything. But then I had my first successes, and they came when I was terribly young. I was only in my early twenties. *The Vortex* opened in London on my twenty-fifth birthday. After that I went through a dangerous phase. Suddenly everything I did became a great success. I didn't realize what danger I was in. I had made this meteoric rise, I had five plays running, I was the belle of the ball—and they got sick of it. And I got careless. I thought it was easy to be a success, and it's never easy.

JUDY: No. No, it never is.

NOEL: I wrote one or two things that weren't so good. And at the age of twenty-seven I found myself booed off the stage by the public on an opening night, and outside the stage door someone spat at me. That was a shock. It didn't hurt me, though. I was rather grateful for the bitter experience, for being shown I wasn't quite as clever as I thought I was.

JUDY: You were grateful to the public?

NOEL: Yes, they judge what they see—and it's up to me to make them see what I want them to see. Now, for instance, last night [the Boston opening of Noel Coward's new play, *Sail Away*] they came into that theater and they got a first impression. I had everything on my side. I had an extremely good cast, very good orchestra, wonderful choreography—

JUDY: And very good music and very good material, darling.

NOEL: Which I'm very proud of. But what was wrong with it—and I know this—was, there are certain moments when it needs tightening. There are certain numbers that occur *here* when they should occur *there*. The first part of the play goes too long without an up number. There are a whole list of lines that might have been hilariously funny but didn't get over, and I've seen it now with two good audiences. So now those lines will be cut, that's what.

JUDY: Gosh, I didn't—I may sound stupid, but I don't remember a good line that anybody missed.

NOEL: There wasn't a *good* line that anybody missed. It was the *bad* lines. (*He laughs*)

JUDY: I don't remember a bad line.

NOEL: Tonight I shall sit in that theater with my secretary and make a note of every line I'm going to cut, and I should think there'll be over fifty. I've already cut four scenes and three big numbers.

JUDY: My God, you're a pro! And that's what's important. You have to know how to make people feel how you want them to feel. That's the challenge. That part that I took in *Judgment in Nuremberg* [*sic*] is a wonderful, wonderful role. It will probably last only about eight minutes on the screen, but what happens in those eight minutes is important, and it was challenging. The whole feeling was challenging—Stanley Kramer, the director, and Spencer Tracy, and a great script. I've always wanted to work with Stanley Kramer. I have a great admiration for him. Why does an actress take a part like that? Because the correct people are involved. Much more important than billing and starring.

NOEL: Billing and starring are the two most boring words in the lexicon. As long as when you're up there you do it right.

JUDY: You were certainly the star last night [at a party for cast and friends after the opening of *Sail Away*].

NOEL: Thank you, darling. There were far too many people there. But I was slightly proud that they had taken that picture of me looking like a very old bull moose and put it up in place of the portrait of George Washington. In Boston, of all places! Considering the Boston Tea Party, this was really very kind of them. I imagine they've forgiven us for that now.

JUDY (*laughing*): At least you've been forgiven.

NOEL: I was absolutely exhausted. I've been working frightfully hard these last few weeks—we had been rehearsing during the day—and then opening night. The first night is always an ordeal. However successful you are, you're always nervous that first night. But it went wonderfully and I was very happy. I came back to the hotel, washed my face and hands, had a drink and then I thought, Now, this must be done properly because everybody is coming to the party. It's my turn to give a performance—at midnight. Then you came. And you stopped being Judy and became *Judy Garland*. And I was no more Noel. I was *Noel Coward*, debonair, witty, charming and . . .

JUDY: . . . and I was Dorothy Adorable.

NOEL: And you were just Dorothy Adorable, and we smiled and we took the show. And there we both were, together with a lot of people who stood around waiting for us to be charming and clever and entertaining. We were such good sorts. My dear, going on being such good sorts in public for a long time is very wearing, because we weren't feeling really in good sorts at all. What we wanted to do is get away and . . .

JUDY: . . . and put on some slacks and sprawl out on the floor.

NOEL: . . . put on some—take off our shoes and have a drink and discuss show business. That's what is really interesting. In all the concerts I did for the troops during the war, the only thing I dreaded was the party given after the show by the commanding officer. I might have done five concerts in a day in the heat of Burma, but the officers would still expect me to come to their party. And then, after giving me a couple of drinks to help me relax, they would come out with it: "How about giving us a few numbers?" You want to clobber them. You're dead. But you say yes.

JUDY: You do it. You do it.

NOEL: You do it. And you go home screaming.

JUDY: I'm getting so I wonder why I do it any more But I still do. I suppose it's something we never—

NOEL: We're show people.

JUDY: I suppose. Once in London, I remember, I was invited to a party. First I had to do some recording, and it took hours. I had five or six recordings, and you know that means doing them over and over—and I sing terribly loud. It was late, and I called and said I'd be late for the party. When I finally arrived, I found that everybody had already eaten and just the leftovers were still on the table—you know, awful bits of cold ham and wilted lettuce. I was so hungry that when the hostess brought me a miserable-looking plate, I started eating. "Now," she said, "Kay [Thompson] is at the piano, and everybody's been waiting for you to sing." I said, "I've just been singing for five hours, you know." But what could I do? Kay and I sang for another three hours. Then we went home on our hands and knees. Just so tired. But the people really were standing like statues and they had been there all evening.

NOEL: They get it for nothing. Getting it for nothing. They say, "Wouldn't it be wonderful if we could persuade her to sing?" That's all right. That's fine. But what is irritating is to be taken for granted, when they expect you to perform come hell or high water. With or without an accompanist, whether or not you've just finished working, you are expected to sing. And as soon as you start—everybody starts to talk.

JUDY: Oh, darling, they don't do that to you too!

NOEL: I'll tell you one little story that happened during the war. I came back to Cairo after a long, hot day entertaining in one hospital after another, and I found a message saying King Farouk was giving a party that evening and would I please come? So I obediently had a shower and got into a white dinner jacket and went off to one of the most boring social affairs imaginable. My eye caught a very nasty-looking upright piano, and I thought, Hello, hello—this is it! And King Farouk, covered in medals, came up and asked me very courteously, "Mr. Coward, would you sing us a few songs?" I thought it discourteous to say that I don't like playing for myself while I sing, so I agreed. I went to the piano and sang a number and everyone was fairly attentive but restless. Then I started on "Night and Day"—I can play it well and I've got a good arrangement. And I did the drip-drip-drip of the raindrops and all the rest, with everyone quiet except King Farouk, who was busy impressing the lady next to him. He was so rude that I lost my temper. So I got to the chorus and sang, "In the roaring traffic's boom . . ." and then I went, "In the SILENCE!" He stopped dead, and there was a terrible hush, and then I continued blithely, ". . . of my lonely room, I think of you."

JUDY (*laughing*): Lovely!

NOEL: In the old days, when we entertainers were considered rogues and vagabonds and we weren't received socially—which of course saved us an enormous amount of boredom—we were bloody well paid for performing. We might be shown in through the servants' quarters, but that was all right. You'd sing your song and get five hundred quid for it.

JUDY: When I was at Metro—I don't think I was much over twelve years old, and they didn't know what to do with me because they wanted you either five years old or eighteen, with nothing in between. Well, I was in between, and so was little Deanna Durbin, and they didn't know what to do with us. So we just went to school every day and wandered around the lot. Whenever the important stars had parties, though, they called the casting office and said "Bring those two kids." We would be taken over and we would wait with the servants until they called us into the drawing room, where we would perform. We never got five hundred quid, though. We got a dish of ice cream—and it would always be melted.

NOEL: But I'm talking about the . . . the big stars now—not kids. In the old days the big stars were common trash, however big the star.

JUDY: With certain groups I still feel that I'm being taken up as a kind of—you know, sort of, oh, it's fun with Judy Garland. She's *fun!* She sings! You feel you're being used as a kind of foolish court jester who'll be dropped next season when the newest property comes in.

NOEL: Oh, yes, and after you've done your number, darling, without any rehearsal and no lighting and no rest, someone says, "My, doesn't he look *old*."

JUDY (*laughing*): Or fat.

NOEL: But, of course, it is no use ever expecting society to understand about show business or entertainers because they never do, do they?

III Misery

Who Is Miss G.?

Picture Studios will soon have to admit that they have an investment in the Dope Racket. Studio Officials must stop running interference for money-loving dishonest doctors, sexual perverts and dipsomaniacs! One Large Major Studio has many glaring examples: sexual perverts, death dealing drunks, dope addicts and other examples of human wreckage.

Miss G. is a talented young famous star. She is also a confirmed dope addict. Her smiling face has turned to a wet one. Her beautiful figure is now a thin shadow. King Dope has decided her fate; she has a habit which is almost incurable.

Who struck Miss G. Down? Who failed to pick her up? What Studio Officials have profited by millions of dollars due to her talent . . . pimps to the great whore, Dope.

—muckraking columnist Jimmie Tarantino
in *Hollywood Night Life,* 1948

Joe Hyams

FROM *PHOTOPLAY*   JANUARY 1957

Crack-Up

A close friend of Judy Garland's recently described her as a cracked plate, still useful but dangerously near the end of its service.

This is the story of the cracks in the plate, of how an exceptionally talented young lady experiences a crack-up of all values, a crack-up she scarcely knew about until long after it occurred.

It is not a pretty story. Some of it has been told before, but no one has ever understood how the gradual building up of tensions, each small within itself, can lead to the crack-up of a great talent.

There is no real beginning because, like the slow, studied dripping of water on stone, tension takes a long time to make an impression. The pressures are always there, because all life is a process of breaking down, but the big blows—the ones that breed nightmares and insomnia and headaches and sessions with psychiatrists—don't show their effects all at once.

The powerful blows are the ones that come from within, like the time Judy was only ten years old and a member of the Gumm Sisters vaudeville act. The family lived in Lancaster, California, a small town where Judy's father managed a movie theatre.

Every weekend Mrs. Gumm gathered up her three girls, took them to Los Angeles and put them onstage for as little as fifty cents per girl per performance, then brought them back home to Lancaster.

"I always felt like a freak in Lancaster," Judy recalled recently. "We were show folks."

Once, when a major charade was being planned, Lancaster social leaders called on the Gumms, borrowed their professional costumes, admired the girls—but didn't invite them to the party. Show business kids were all right as entertainers but not as social equals.

That was the first time Judy Garland was made aware she was "different." It was not the last.

When she was twelve her mother and father separated. Judy was the baby of the family—she was even called Baby—and the apple of her father's eye. She never understood why he left her.

When she was thirteen Judy enrolled at Hollywood High School. A vice-principal who was to be one of her teachers came over and said, "People like you should not be allowed to go to school with normal children."

In those days Judy was as round as a ball, with just as much bounce. She was pretty, with large brown eyes, a farm-fresh complexion and a puppy-dog personality. She was, she believed, as normal as blueberry pie, certainly as normal as any other little girl of thirteen.

What do you say to a teacher who tells you you're not normal, don't belong with normal children? Judy said nothing. But she was so upset she never returned to the school. Instead she enrolled at a private school with other "professional children."

Dorothy Gray, a child star in those days and Judy's best friend, remembers her as Baby Gumm, the prettiest girl in her class, popularly conceded to be the most talented.

"Judy and I did all the things little girls do, from making fudge to roller skating," Dorothy recalled. "But whenever we went to the movies we had to leave our names at the box office in case we got a studio call.

"There were a lot of things we couldn't do, like take regular vacations or go swimming, because we might miss a film call or catch a cold.

"We theatrical kids used to be embarrassed when our pictures were in the paper because the other—normal—kids we knew would tease us. I guess in a way we were robbed of childhood. Only two or three in the whole group we grew up with and worked with haven't turned out as drunks, neurotics or bad-check passers."

Judy's father died the year she was signed by M-G-M. Her mother, Mrs. Gumm, was then put on the studio payroll, and began to use the studio as a disciplinary threat in the place of Judy's father. This was to have a lifelong effect on Judy's emotional make-up and to color all her later relationships with M-G-M.

"You behave, Judy, or I'll tell the studio on you," Mrs. Gumm would say. Judy became afraid of "the studio," the place where she spent most of her waking time.

"There were thumb screws inside me every time I walked on the lot," Judy said recently, recalling those years. "The atmosphere at M-G-M was one of terror. My life for a time was full of fear. Going into the studio was like going to a haunted house every day."

What was it like to have a major motion picture studio for a parent? If one incident can be cited as an example of a blow from within, here it is:

Judy made twelve pictures in her teens. She had to dance, cry and act before the cameras, in addition to singing. Like all professional children under contract to a major studio, she also had to sandwich in six hours of school every day. The only thing Judy could do that she liked was to eat. At every meal she stuffed herself with all the food she could cram in, sneaked in double malts between scenes, nibbled on chocolate bars at school—and gained weight. Finally an M-G-M executive sent for her.

"You look like a hunchback," he told her. "We love you but you're so fat you look like a monster." Judy tried to smile through the tears, then ran. At the time she was called a monster she was violently in love with Clark Gable.

After this incident a humiliating directive was sent down from the front office. No matter what Judy ordered for lunch she was to be given only a small bowl of consommé. The studio's attitude is completely understandable. They had a movie star under contract, a movie to be made, millions of stockholders' dollars tied up in it. They were completely sympathetic with Judy's emotional problems—problems which she had tried to solve with the temporary relief of overeating. On the other hand, Judy had contracted to make a picture and the picture had to be made.

From then on lunch time became a cruel game for Judy. Hungry from working hard all morning, she would go to the studio commissary, sit at a table by herself and order a full meal. The waitress would take the order, then return with a bowl of broth. Judy would smile bravely through the tears and sip her lunch. She always ate alone.

And, while sipping her lunch, Judy more than once would overhear someone in the commissary point her out as "that little girl they were stuck with when they let Deanna Durbin go."

*   *   *

Judy was famous and a star but she was miserable. A friend described her as a "toy money machine which could be wound up and set to work in the morning, turned off at night, and put on a shelf just like any other toy. She was never treated as a person."

Once, Judy's older sister, Suzanne, brought her small daughter out to the studio for lunch. "Isn't it wonderful?" said Suzanne. "I'd like my little girl to be a movie star, too." Judy almost screamed at her. She pounded the table and yelled, "I'll break your neck if you ever bring the child to the studio again!"

That was one of the first indications that the pressures were forcing a crack in the pottery of Judy's personality.

Judy's friends insist that she never wanted to be a movie star at all. She merely wanted to sing. But from the beginning Judy's pictures were big spectacles, requiring long rehearsals and recording sessions, dancing and acting as well as singing. Judy threw herself completely into everything she did. Even in those days she was a perfectionist and gave it everything she had.

A director who knew her then said, "Judy should have done just one scene a day, then taken an ambulance home."

Once, while doing a dance routine, she almost collapsed. "I'm so tired and I'm so hungry," she gasped to the director. He replied, "Do this routine again and you'll forget you're hungry."

Judy got tired from overworking and undereating. To keep herself going she started to take a stimulant called Benzedrine. Then she had to take sleeping pills to counteract the Benzedrine and let her sleep, and then more pills to wake her up. Judy says of this time, "I lived on bolts and jolts."

The sleepless nights and hungry days began to have an effect on Judy. She became nervous, irritable and ill. One day she didn't show up for work and the entire studio was in an uproar. For the first time in her life Judy began to realize that she was something of a personage. She was genuinely ill, but she found that people considered her illness "temperament," a not unusual occurrence in Hollywood. Though annoyed, people really began to pay attention to her, and Judy began to bask in the realization that she was, at long last, important.

Coupled with the weakening of her physical structure she had discovered a test which enabled her to learn if people really cared for her. Like a child who thinks herself unloved, Judy began to kick up her heels just to assure herself that everyone loved her.

A psychiatrist would call this an infantile regression, a search for the affection she missed as a child. The diagnosis would probably be accurate. After her father's death Judy spent most of her time searching for the affection and attention that the corporate entity which had, to all intents and purposes, become her parents was unable to give her.

The crack was getting larger.

By the time Judy was sixteen she had become a singing workhorse. She threw herself into every production with her whole heart and body and as a result was burned out after every picture. Between pictures she rested by reading scripts for her next one.

"They never gave me a rest," she complains now of those years. "I went from picture to picture. They would promise me a six-month vacation, but after I had been away a week or two they would call me back again.

"I'd start a new picture, then break down. There would be rows and suspensions. We would try to straighten it out, but when I went back to work the whole thing started over again."

We must remember that Judy's studio was faced with the fact that they were dealing with an emotionally sick and exhausted person—one who refused, like the fighter she is, to lie down.

By now, Judy was beginning to realize that her life was no longer her own. Even worse, she earned $5,000 a week, $150,000 a picture, but had nothing to show for it. Her mother had been appointed guardian of her money, but most of it was spent as fast as it came in. How much was spent on legitimate living expenses for Judy and how much might have been unnecessary extravagance is something that was later to be investigated through legal procedures. Meanwhile, all Judy had to show for the large sums she had earned was a small trust fund which the courts had insisted be put aside.

Judy exhausted herself trying to keep up with Mickey Rooney, the Whiz Kid of movies. She became a big star herself with *The Wizard of Oz*. In 1939, when *Oz* opened in New York, she went with Mickey to make a personal appearance at the Capitol Theatre.

They broke records doing six and seven shows a day at forty-five minutes a show, with only forty minutes between each appearance. One day, as they finished the set and went off stage, Judy collapsed in the wings. She had been working too hard and too fast without letting up.

Judy had hit emotional high gear. It was at this point that she met David Rose, the composer and orchestra leader. He was serious, preoccupied and older.

Everyone in Hollywood has a theory about why Judy married him. Most people think it was rebellion against work. Some say she thought orchestra life would be more Bohemian and fun. Judy says simply, "He was good to me."

The marriage was short; it lasted only four years. As compensation for her unhappiness Judy again turned to food. M-G-M rightly insisted she lose weight. Extreme in everything she did, Judy took to starvation diets of black coffee and cigarettes which, coupled with work, exhausted her even more. The answer: more stimulants, more sleeping pills.

By 1945 Judy was no longer employable. She was world-famous, hungry, sleepy, divorced and unhappy, and she held up productions, a cardinal sin in Hollywood. She dropped out of *The Barkleys of Broadway* and was replaced by Ginger Rogers. That night she stayed at M-G-M, crying in her dressing room, protesting that no one loved her.

But a week after her divorce from David Rose she married director Vincente Minnelli. This marriage lasted on and off for nearly six years.

Suddenly Judy began to have a strong feeling that she must be alone, that she didn't want to see any people at all. After her daughter Liza was born she was in a weakened condition, and her prodigious appetite left her for the first time. She lived on nervous energy and doctors' prescriptions.

When Hedda Hopper visited her on the set of *The Pirate,* Judy took the columnist into the dressing room and went into a frenzy, saying everyone was against her, that she had no friends. After that she began to fail to show up for work and she was suspended.

She pleaded with M-G-M to let her work, so they have her in *In the Good Old Summertime.* She finished it on schedule and the studio rewarded her with its biggest picture, *Annie Get Your Gun.*

The director, Arthur Freed, had been with Judy in the old days, but she demanded he be replaced. The nerves and exhaustion were showing again. She recorded her songs, then started rehearsals. One day at lunch hour she went home and didn't return. The studio announced that she had been suspended and Betty Hutton was signed to replace her.

Judy was broke, off salary and jobless. She was convinced nobody cared for her.

She was twenty-seven years old when the first big crack appeared. A person can crack in many ways: in the head, in which case the power of decision is taken away from you by others; in the body; or in the nerves. It was Judy's nervous reflexes that gave way, the result of too much work and too many tears.

Now, the studio once more assumed the role of parent. Louis B. Mayer, head of M-G-M, sent her to the Peter Bent Brigham Hospital in Boston and paid the bill. Carlton Alsop, the man Judy calls "Pa," recalls her convalescence: "I used to take her out for trial runs, to baseball games, to see how she reacted. Then, I'd take her shopping. There was always a car handy, so that if she had a relapse we could rush her back."

While in Boston, Mr. Alsop took Judy to a little summer theatre. When the word got around that she was in the audience, the cast asked her to join them in a farewell backstage party. Judy accepted. After the paying customers had gone home the cast serenaded Judy from the stage, then asked her to sing to them

She turned to Mr. Alsop and asked, "Pa, do you think I have any voice?" He told her she still had the best voice in show business. He told her to try singing. She did—and sang for forty minutes.

"Judy found she hadn't lost her voice," Mr. Alsop recalled. "It was medicine she couldn't get in the hospital."

Judy stayed in the hospital eleven weeks, at last started to sleep regularly, and gained weight.

Then the studio called her back for *Summer Stock,* produced by Judy's old friend, Joe Pasternak. Again she was "too fat." In addition, she wasn't well enough to be working, but she needed the money and the studio needed her, so she raced to reduce before going back on the set.

To help in the dieting Judy once again started on pills, first to reduce, then to help her sleep and forget the pangs of hunger. One day she failed to show up for work and was threatened with suspension. She was told there were three million dollars riding on her and that she was being temperamental and selfish. Studio people were given orders to watch her every minute. A specialist was flown out from Boston to be in readiness on the set "just in case."

Somehow Judy finished *Summer Stock* and, although promised a vacation, went right into *Royal Wedding.* This one she never finished. One Saturday morning she failed to show up. The studio called four times and was told she was on the way, but she never left home. The studio suspended her and announced Jane Powell as her replacement.

In the presence of four friends, including Mr. Alsop and her husband, Vincente Minnelli, Judy tried to cut her throat. It was a feeble attempt, but to Judy it represented something.

She said, "All I could see ahead was more confusion. I wanted to black out the future as well as the past. I wanted to hurt myself and everyone else."

Judy had reached the bottom of her emotional reserve. She had mortgaged herself physically and spiritually. But the response of her fans was amazing. She received hundreds of telegrams from fans wishing her well. The only one she saw was from Freddie Finkelhoffe, the songwriter, who said "Dear Judy. So glad you cut your throat. All the other singers needed the break."

Mr. Alsop, who received the wire, took it in to Judy. She laughed hysterically at it. "They still love me, don't they," she said to Alsop.

Katharine Hepburn came by while Judy was convalescing and delivered a long speech about how important Judy was, not only to herself, but to those whom she had brought so much pleasure. Judy listened quietly and then made up her mind to get back on her feet.

"I grabbed my daughter, Liza, and moved into a seven-room suite at the Beverly Hills Hotel," Judy recalls. "When we had been there a few weeks and I thought they might start asking about the bill, I packed a couple of cases, dashed down to the desk and told them I had just been called to New York and would they save my suite for me. "It was a big bluff, but they never thought to question it. We flew to New York and I did the same thing there. Of course it was mad, but it was the first real fun I had had in my life. I had worked like a dog and I was broke—but I was beginning to be happy. I was free."

The crack in her personality was being mended.

In New York Judy did all the things she had never been allowed to do before. She stuffed herself with food, went window-shopping, went to bed and got up when she pleased.

The long-term contract with M-G-M was dissolved at Judy's request. This left her alone, separated from her mother, who Judy felt had let her down, and on the verge of divorce from Minnelli.

Her reputation for unpredictable and expensive behavior was so widely publicized that no producer wanted to take a chance on her.

Judy tried to run away from herself and Hollywood by going to Europe, where she ate herself into obscurity. When she returned to Hollywood a year later, all washed up at twenty-eight, she met Sid Luft at a party. It was Luft who suggested she regain her confidence in herself by opening at the London Palladium.

Then Judy began the weary drudge on the long road back. If there are pressures which can crack, there are also incidents which can heal. Sometimes the person is the stronger for having broken and been patched together properly.

On the night of April 10, 1951, when Judy Garland opened at the Palladium, she began to patch herself up. Here for the first time is her story of that night. She said:

"The night before the opening, I didn't sleep a wink. I was terror-stricken. At daybreak I was pacing up and down my hotel room, almost out of my mind with panic and fear. I kept rushing to the bathroom to vomit. I couldn't eat, I couldn't sleep. I couldn't even sit down.

"When they finally got me to the dressing room I was only half-conscious. I hadn't worked at all for almost three years, and had given a show in public barely once or twice since I was a kid.

"There were only minutes left. I had to get hold of myself. I said to myself, 'What's the matter, you dope? If you don't cut this out you won't be able to sing. Don't worry. They won't eat you.'

"Standing in the wings, waiting to go on, I became paralyzed. My knees locked together and I walked on like a stiff-legged toy soldier. And after a while, without knowing how it had happened, I found myself, not standing on the stage, but sitting on it. It was said I tripped over a wire or a loose board. That's not true. I didn't fall at all, really. I just collapsed.

"The fall happened after I had sung two or three numbers. I was trying to take a bow. I just went 'Ugh' and sat down. I sat there and thought, 'Damn this.' I looked up at Sid, who was hanging out of a box, screaming, 'You're great, baby, you're great!'

"Somehow I got back on my feet, lurched back to the wings. I remember thinking, 'That's it. Judy falls on her can and that's the end of the great comeback.'

"I was ready to quit, but my old friend Kay Thompson was waiting at the side of the stage. She screamed, 'Get back there. They love you.' Then she gave me a hug and a shove that carried me back almost to the center stage.

"Instead of giving me the bird, those wonderful British people clasped me to their hearts. I unlocked, and everything I wanted to do came surging out. All the bad years went. It was like being reborn. It was like being given a new life to start all over again."

Later that year, Judy brought vaudeville back to the Palace Theater in New York. She was overweight again and, naturally, she collapsed from overwork. But she rested a few days and returned to enjoy a record-breaking run of nineteen weeks. Night after night, audiences called out the old refrain, "Judy, we love you."

Sid and Judy brought the show to Los Angeles and another tearful, thrilling triumph. That spring she and Luft were married. At last it appeared that Judy had lived up to the words of her most famous song. Somewhere over the rainbow, she had found happiness. The happiness was short lived.

Judy's relations with her mother broke into court. Her mother had married a man named William Gilmore, whom Judy did not admire. It has already been stated that Judy felt her mother had mishandled her finances.

Mrs. Gilmore went to court to complain that Judy would not support her. She took a job as a sixty-dollar-a-week clerk at Douglas Aircraft. Judy's friends, who recall that Mrs. Gilmore was a first-rate piano and singing teacher (she taught Judy, among others) think she took the job just to embarrass her daughter.

Judy's daughter, Lorna Luft, was born December 8, 1952. Less than a month later Judy's mother fell dead in a Los Angeles parking lot.

Judy, who had thought she was better, cracked like an old plate when she heard the news. For two years she was "in sanitaria," her term for psychiatric treatment. She did no work, saw very few people. When she finally emerged it was to make *A Star Is Born* at Warners.

Hollywood biographer Cameron Shipp notes that she "approached this as fearfully as a child in the dark."

"She was terrified," said Sid Luft. "She hadn't make a picture in nearly four years. She thought she was through, washed up, all over again. That's why she made the picture so difficult."

And difficult it was. Cary Grant, who was all but set as Judy's leading man, was replaced by James Mason; five cameramen and four costume designers walked off or were fired from the job; a musical arranger left in a huff; the set was closed to the press for most of the shooting; the budget, first estimated at $2,000,000, was more than doubled; and the picture had the longest consistent shooting schedule of any picture in recent Hollywood history.

Judy said little other than that she is a perfectionist. And so is Sid. "We *had* to have it right. We *had* to take time. Of course, there were rows and friction. There is in every picture that's worth anything. We all did our share, but I was the bull's-eye in the target and everybody aimed straight at me."

When the time for the 1955 Oscars came around, everyone was certain Judy would get the Best Actress award for her performance in *A Star Is Born*. She did not. Grace Kelly won it for her work in *The Country Girl*.

A few hours before the award was announced, Judy was in the hospital giving birth to Joseph Luft, her second child by Sid. Everyone said her failure to win an Oscar would crack her wide open—for once and always.

Surprisingly, it didn't. Somehow Judy had repurchased the spiritual and physical mortgage she had given in exchange for stardom as a child. At last she had inner resources to draw on. One such resource was humor.

With mime and words she tells of the hospital scene on the night she found out she hadn't won the Oscar.

"Just picture it," says Judy. "There I was, weak and exhausted after the battle to bring Joe into the world. He wasn't in such good shape, either; at that moment doctors didn't give him better than a fifty-fifty chance.

"I was lying in bed, trying to get my breath back, when the door burst open and in came a flock of television technicians. I already had a TV set on, but they dragged in two more huge ones. I asked what they were for and they said that after I got the award I would have to talk back and forth to Bob Hope, who was emceeing.

"They strung wires all around the room. They put a microphone under my nightgown. They frightened the poor nurse to death when they told her, 'If you open that window while the show is on we'll kill you.'

"Then they built a four-story-high tower outside the hospital, for cameras which were to focus through the window. What with all the excitement and everything, they got me all worked up, too. I was flat on my back in bed, trying to look cute.

"I was all ready to give a performance. Then Bob Hope came on the screen and said Grace Kelly had won.

"I'll never forget it to my dying day. The technicians in my room said, 'Kelly! Aah,' then started lugging all the stuff out again. You should have seen the looks on their faces as they tramped out with all that gear. I really thought I would have hysterics."

Sid had brought three bottles of champagne and a dish of caviar with which to celebrate with Judy after she had won the Oscar. When the TV men had gone he said, "How do you feel?" Judy said, "Disappointed."

That night they sat alone, sipping the champagne and eating the caviar. But Judy remembers the night with a smile that has a twinkle—not hurt—shining through.

Judy seems at long last to have learned to live with herself. That doesn't mean she has become people-broken and docile. She still is a perfectionist, who insists on absolute perfection in everything she does. And, she still needs to know that everyone loves her.

In September 1955, for example, while she was rehearsing for her first television appearance, the director, Paul Harrison, called all of the technicians into a huddle. He told them about Judy. "She's a child," he said. "If you mention that her nose is shiny she's likely to walk off the set and not go on at all. Be careful of everything you do and say around her, but remember she's one of the greatest talents any of you will ever work with. For the next four days keep that in mind and love her. If you do nothing else, make her know you love her."

Despite the pep talk, rehearsals for the show were not all smooth. Judy came late, keeping three color-camera crews idle at $1,200 an hour. It took six hours to film two 20-second promotion teasers for the show, which should normally have been done in fifteen minutes. Even on the day of dress rehearsal, Judy was forty-five minutes late.

But the ninety-minute *Ford Star Jubilee* for CBS-TV had the largest viewing audience ever to watch a spectacular. For CBS-TV, the end justified the means. And that, to a large extent, is the story of Judy's personal life.

Ever since she was a child, people have put up with Judy's erratic behavior because they believe talent is a law unto itself. And as long as she continues as one of the world's great attractions she'll be judged by a unique set of rules.

Last summer, Judy completed a five-week run at the New Frontier Hotel in Las Vegas, where she made her nightclub debut. She was paid $35,000 a week, while the hotel paid an additional $20,000 a week for the orchestra and other acts. The previous high for an entire show had been $50,000 for Liberace. Judy insisted on being the highest-paid entertainer. Her thinking was, "If they want me they'll have to pay me," and the fact that they were willing to go so high proved to her that they truly did want her.

As always, she missed performances and made irritating demands on the hotel proprietors, but she brought in large enough crowds to give the hotel a profit.

Judy wanted to play in Las Vegas for the most elemental reason. She said, "I have to get money to pay off back taxes."

Despite the fact that she is one of the world's greatest entertainers, she is almost broke. Although the Lufts live in a big home, it is virtually unfurnished, for a big star Judy has a remarkably small wardrobe, and she and Sid have no money in the bank. Today, all Judy has to show for sixteen years at M-G-M is a scarred psyche, a paid-up $100,000 insurance policy and a pitifully small income from the one investment left over from her childhood.

Even without material things the Lufts seem happy. Their entire home is planned to permit their children—Lorna, 4, Joseph, 21 months, and Liza, 10—to have freedom to play, The extensive outside grounds are covered with playground equipment and children's toys. There is no swimming pool because it would be a menace to the children.

"We haven't bothered to furnish the house completely," Judy says. "We believe the house should grow with us. We aren't through growing yet and neither is the house. If I have my way (despite doctor's orders) we'll have a few more kids around. It's children, not furniture, that make the home."

In her home Judy is as unlike a star as anyone could imagine. On a recent visit to her home this writer found the children very well adjusted to each other. They seemed at ease with both parents and are all treated equally.

On one occasion, when Liza interrupted a conversation to ask her mother a question, Judy very quietly told her we were talking and would she mind waiting a minute.

A moment later, we finished our conversation. Judy turned to Liza, saying "Now, darling, what was it you wanted to say to me?"

Then baby Joseph toddled into the room in his pajamas. He clambered up on Judy's knee while we talked. When it was time for his supper Judy smothered him with kisses and said, "You're the nicest baby in the world and I love you."

Obviously, Judy has no intention of neglecting her children as she was neglected as a child.

During the week Judy was rehearsing twelve hours a day for her night-club act, recording an album for Capitol Records and staying up all night with Joseph, who had a temperature of 104.5° for two days. In the evening she prepared dinner for the family while the nurse rested.

But you can't explain all this to an audience which pays to see a performance, and Judy knows it. Bleary-eyed and tired, she went on in Las Vegas, and the few shows she missed were probably the result of genuine fatigue.

But on opening night she was surrounded by her entire family, brought in by train for the event. And she seemed happy.

"In the old days I was overworked and exhausted and had no idea of what I was punishing myself for," she said. "I had no place to go and nothing that mattered and no goal.

"Now, when I get through work I'm still exhausted, but I go home at night to my family and forget about everything else. I have a full personal life besides a full professional life. One balances the other."

In addition, Judy seems to have a good marriage with Sid Luft, despite occasional quarrels which apparently serve to clear the air between them. However, the cracks in Judy's personality are still there, only temporarily mended. As long as she stays in show business she can expect to be on the receiving end of the strong blows which forced her out in the past.

Recently, Judy returned to the Palace Theater in New York where, again, she emerged as Queen. The superlatives lavished on her were necessary to keep her going. In one of her rare moments of self-analysis she told a friend what it means to her to be a success, why it was necessary.

"When people go on telling you for years that you are washed up, finished, you begin to think maybe they're right," Judy told her friend. "Then you sit down and think that if you once had talent, maybe you still have it.

"So you work, work, work to polish it up again and you try and go on trying. Finally you are as ready as you can be to go before the public again.

"On opening night you are sure you are crazy. You suffer and you writhe. You know you are not going to be able to sing a note. You know nobody is going to like you. All those tales about you being no good keep going through your head and you wonder why you ever got into this again.

"The curtain goes up and you totter onstage, half stupefied with nerves.

You barely know what you are doing. It isn't until that first applause comes crashing up that you get any relief. They go on clapping and you are so happy you want to cry and hug everyone down there. You're not finished. You're still Judy Garland—and they still like you. And you think, like a prayer, God bless all of you for understanding."

Richard Warren Lewis

FROM *THE SATURDAY EVENING POST*   DECEMBER 7, 1963

The TV Troubles of Judy Garland

Within a control booth at CBS Television City in Hollywood nestles broadcasting's first actual panic button. If pushed, the button will trigger a deafening din of tape-recorded cannon fire, horns, whistles, sirens, bomb blasts, bells, chimes and machine gun bursts over the public address system of Studio 43, site of the weekly *Judy Garland Show*. The tape stands at the ready for a reason: as a facetious method of quieting the sometimes temperamental Miss Garland should she have an emotional outburst.

But the button has never been pushed. Outwardly, at least, Judy has displayed remarkable control while her TV show has been turbulent. Trumpeted in advance as one of the season's powerhouse programs, the Garland hour has thus far ranked as one of its major disappointments. It has been plagued offstage by spotty reviews and low ratings, and backstage by petty politicking, confusion and bickering. "This show is the *Cleopatra* of television," says the program's former executive producer, Norman Jewison.

When Miss Garland signed a multi-million-dollar TV contract last spring, some observers were skeptical about her survival. Despite her extraordinary string of concert successes, nightclub sellouts and TV specials, the singer's durability was a question mark. In the previous year she had been stricken by a kidney ailment. She also collapsed during a nightclub engagement, winding up in a Nevada hospital, a victim of complete physical exhaustion.

Furthermore, Miss Garland, 41, had a history of missing cues, forgetting lyrics, skipping rehearsals, collapsing on stage and losing her voice. Her marital troubles, weight problems, insomnia and financial straits have been public knowledge for years. "Thousands of dollars were bet in Las Vegas that I wouldn't even do the first three shows," Judy now admits with a laugh. "They thought that I wasn't going to finish a performance or even show up."

It was with some trepidation that several hundred representatives of stations affiliated with the CBS network assembled last May to see their million-dollar baby firsthand. On the flight to New York, Judy was almost as wary. She was accompanied by her producer, George Schlatter, who had won Judy's favor when they met by joking, "I want you to know that there is no truth to the rumor that I'm difficult."

Together Schlatter and Judy composed a special song parody designed to disarm the affiliates. Stepping on stage in a Manhattan ballroom, Judy softened up the station heads by deadpanning new words to the song hit, "Call Me Irresponsible". "Call me irresponsible, call me unreliable," she quavered, "but it's undeniably true, I'm irrevocably signed with you." The gathering stood up and cheered.

And for the first weeks of production, Judy lived up to the lyrics. Her voice was firm and clear. She had slimmed down to 100 pounds, a marked contrast to her former pudginess. She rarely missed a rehearsal. In fact, she showed up at the studio even when she was not scheduled to appear. "She was really swinging with it, and we were all swinging together," recalls Bill Hobin.

Her good spirits were aided by the unusual creature comforts requisitioned for her by Schlatter. A 40-by-10-foot house trailer, air-conditioned and emblazoned with red and white candy stripes, was hoisted to a second floor ramp and converted into her dressing room. Behind the trailer's kissing-cupids door knocker, an interior decorator created a miniature replica of the star's home, complete with wall-to-wall carpeting, antique marble tables and indirect pink lighting. The furnishings included a piano, stereophonic sound system, tape recorder, serving bar and a refrigerator containing Judy's favorite wine, Blue Nun Liebfraumilch.

Nearly $100,000 was spent on studio facilities. The stage was raised, a separate revolving stage was imbedded in the floor and workmen created a battery of Marconi television cameras—the latest electronic marvels which magically remove wrinkles from faces. To brighten the short walk along the drab hallway from dressing room to stage door, workmen painted a winding yellow brick path, reminiscent of the magic road in Judy's smash hit *The Wizard of Oz.*

She was having a ball

When her guest stars were before the cameras, Judy encouraged them like a carefree schoolgirl, bouncing around out of camera range and leading the audience's applause. Often, blasé technicians, stagehands and control-room occupants would break into unabashed cheers after one of Judy's own numbers. "She was having a ball," recalls Schlatter. Sponsors approved the shows. Advertising agencies lauded them. Things looked so bright that director Hobin, whose deal with the network included shipment of his family of three and his three-gaited show horse to the West Coast, put his house in Scarsdale, N.Y., up for sale.

But, oddly enough, the mood was not optimistic in New York. CBS executives, led by President James Aubrey Jr., viewed the first three taped shows with some apprehension. The brass believed that the programs lacked a feeling of pattern. "Any weekly show has to be formatted," said CBS Vice President Hunt Stromberg Jr. "There have to be standard compartments that audiences look forward to, like Garry Moore's 'That Wonderful Year.'" There was also concern over Judy's lack of contact with the viewer. "It's important that the audience should not be afraid to like the star," said Stromberg. "Judy was too unreachable."

George Schlatter thought differently. "Since Garland is one of the few giants," he explains, "I felt her show required a different kind of television. I wanted each show to be a special event and to tape it as a live theatrical presentation. I couldn't do a show with tracing paper."

Nevertheless, Schlatter followed orders. In the fourth show he added a segment where Judy sat in a camp chair and chatted with one of her guests, Terry Thomas, over a cup of tea. He created a nostalgic, "I Was Born in a Trunk" section in which Judy pulled objects from a steamer trunk, reminisced about her show business past and sang old songs.

While Schlatter was making these changes, CBS—without Judy's knowledge—ran a series of tests on the completed shows in various parts of the country. Citizens were recruited at random, led into darkened studios, and shown the programs on giant screens. Their impressions of Judy were registered on electronic reaction devices and on written comment cards. "Nobody judged the show," says one observer of the test results. "They judged what they were reading about Garland in the newspapers. On the cards, they commented on what they knew, not what they saw. They said things like, 'I don't like her, she's nervous,' 'She seems unhappy' or 'She drinks.' They felt she was hiding her real self."

CBS officials studied the reactions, considered the network's big investment in the show and lowered the boom. First to go was Schlatter, who seems to have erred in trying to produce a show too original for the network's and perhaps the average viewer's taste. "We are delighted with the five shows that have been completed by Schlatter and deeply regret the difference of opinion as to the course of future productions on the show," said CBS Vice President Richard Lewine. Three writers and a choreographer were also dismissed in the purge.

"Everybody went," Judy recalls. "I thought I was going, too. They swept out a whole bunch of people and whoever got caught up in that whisk of the broom was out. I wish somebody would have warned me in advance—maybe I could have avoided anyone's being decapitated. I was stunned and bewildered. It came as such a shock."

To revamp the show CBS resorted to its checkbook. Writers Arne Sultan and Marvin Worth were hired at $10,000 a week. Diminutive Norman Jewison, who had directed an award-winning Garland TV special in 1962, was brought in for $12,500 a week as chief troubleshooter and named executive producer. The added costs of paying off the old group and hiring the new ones at inflated salaries swelled each show's budget from about $155,000 to an estimated $200,000.

Jewison flew to Hollywood from a vacation in the Canadian backwoods, slipped into an initialed broadcloth shirt and a sincere rep tie, and immediately found what was wrong. "The audience only knows Judy Garland through what they've read in the paper, that she's fat or she's skinny and she drinks," he said, parroting what the tests already had shown. "This kind of publicity, some of it possibly true, has been a product of the Hollywood grist mills. People don't really know Judy Garland. On television you go into millions of homes and actually expose yourself as a personality. That's how we got to know Jack Paar and Perry Como.

"Perry's writers made him the laziest man in television. They created Frank Gallup, who used to put Como down a little and took him off his pedestal. Soon the audience recognized that Perry was a warm, human man.

We had to do the same thing with Judy. The first thing I said to her was, 'Let's be honest, absolutely honest. I love it when you say, "Yeah, I used to be fat."' Are you supposed to hide that? Many people have a weight problem. I thought Judy should be allowed to express herself."

The new writers also echoed the network line. "Television is a habit," Sultan said. "You can't be an event every week. If you do five shows that are each different, you are dead. There's got to be some sameness. If we had that, maybe we'd win some of the Art Linkletter–type fans. That's what keeps you on the air."

To determine what they could learn from existing TV successes, the new team halted production for five weeks. "By stopping the momentum built up in the first five shows, they took a big gamble," says one member of the show. "But after that break, Judy seemed to sort of fall apart and has never come out of it. She never recovered from the shock of being told the show wasn't good."

"Judy just seemed unhappy because she didn't quite understand what was going on," Jewison explains. "They had told her she was just marvelous, the show was just wonderful, when possibly it could have been better. She was confused and slightly depressed." Three weeks after the upheaval Judy entered Cedars of Lebanon hospital briefly for what was described as her "annual checkup." When she reported to the set after production resumed, those working on the show soon sensed a change in her.

The first hour taped under Jewison's helm costarred June Allyson, Judy's sidekick in post-war M-G-M musicals. For the program they sang tunes from movies like *Words and Music* and *Till the Clouds Roll By*. Perhaps the memories of the good old days at Metro affected both of them. According to several members of the show, there was some drinking both before and after the taping.

The levity grew even livelier after the audience went home. A gooey cake was wheeled out to celebrate singer Mel Tormé's 38th birthday. Miss Allyson grabbed the cake and pantomimed throwing it in his face. She chased him around the stage, cake cocked. Somehow the confection fell to the floor, which set off an icing-slinging contest among Garland, Allyson and two friends that smacked of a Mack Sennett two reeler.

Although Judy is generally keyed up for a performance and has a tendency to slur her lines, observers thought they noticed more slurred lines than usual when she was talking to the audience or trading chatter with June. Partly for production reasons and partly because the show as a whole was somewhat sloppy, the director found it necessary to mix portions of the actual show with pieces of the taped dress rehearsal to flesh out a full hour of programming.

Judy, however, pooh-poohs the report that drinking may have affected her performance the night Miss Allyson appeared. "I never in my life have had too much to drink—when I work or when I don't work," she says. "I really don't drink that much and neither does June." As for the icing-slinging incident, she says, "That was just silliness."

In the ensuing weeks, Judy began missing some rehearsals, according to several members of the show. Judy denies this. "I haven't missed any re-hearsals," she says. "If I had, I wouldn't have been able to do the show. There's no time to indulge yourself on weekly television—you don't even have time to get a headache or catch a cold." Nevertheless, one former member of the cast says she did play occasional hooky and elaborates: "Her not coming in for rehearsal has got to be a disadvantage. Nobody really knows what's happening without her. I never really got to rehearse my lines enough."

To which, Jewison adds: "Look, if you want somebody who's gonna be right on time and attend every rehearsal, go work with Dinah Shore. I admit that Judy isn't known for arriving on time. She'll always be there a little late. But I have never met anyone in my life who can pick up a routine as quickly."

An embittered member of the orchestra puts it differently. "If you're writing about Garland," he said, "tell her to get to rehearsal on time."

His advice underscores the morale on the program, which seems to be sagging. "This is a disorganized operation," admits one member of the pro-duction crew. "Oftentimes I don't even know what the shows are about when I go into rehearsal. And then they keep changing. Each revision in our scripts is printed on a different color of paper. A script looks like a rainbow by the time you get finished. Once we ran out of colors and went back to white paper for the tenth revision. I'd like to have the paper concession."

Already, four different choreographers have worked for the show. One program was two and a half hours late because of a debate in Miss Garland's dressing room over how several numbers should be done. The lengthy delay had a decided effect on the studio audience present for the taping. "It was deadly," recalls one observer. "You get a lot of older people who come; it's past their bedtime by the time the show starts and they're tired. They don't laugh at anything." As a result, laugh and applause tracks are liberally laced into shows with the audience's real reactions. "Most shows that have been on the air, we've sweetened," says a member of the production staff. "That's just the general policy, to sweeten everything."

Insiders on the show lately detect another Garland defect. "She comes across on screen as a fidgety, scared little gal," says one of them. "There's this frenetic quality. And an apparent need for contact with guest stars, both men and women. She's just too affectionate. She paws them, touches them and kisses them." The trade paper *Variety* noted: "[She is] so unable to control her gestures of admiration and affection for [her guests], that it all comes out terribly insincere and tends to make viewers cringe."

"I don't see anything objectionable about it," says Judy in reply. "If I think someone is funny, I'll laugh and touch them. If guests are nervous, the nicest thing to do is put an arm around them."

"She used to appear much more relaxed and happier," is another common observation. "She wasn't as jumpy or nervous." Now down to 94 pounds, Judy is sometimes so keyed up she eats no food for the 36 hours before a taping. "I always need a certain amount of excitement and tension to work well," is Judy's explanation. "I'm not the type of performer who can relax and put her feet up and get paid all that money. It's not nerves. Maybe it's just a kind of exuberance, which I've always had."

Sometimes for technical reasons and occasionally because of voice problems, many of Garland's songs have to be taped in advance. What viewers frequently see is Judy moving her lips to a prerecorded sound track. This is unhappily apparent when her lips fail to match the sound track exactly. "I think," says Judy laughingly, "I've been singing *Japanese Sandman* when I was supposed to sing *It's a Good Day*." She also reads lyrics, jokes and dialogue for the bulk of the show off cue cards, memory aids often detrimental to the spontaneity which is Judy's hallmark. And under Jewison, she endured an Orwellian method for learning new material. "We constantly play the tapes in her trailer," he once said, "so she'll get that phrasing. She has to work on it for a long time."

Under the new regime, there has been a strong attempt to pull Judy away from that group of devotees known as "the cult." The cult consists of those boosters who have made her one-woman concerts standing room only, have broken through police lines to be near her, and have bought 420,000 copies of her two-record Carnegie Hall LP. "Members of the cult don't want to share her," according to writer Worth. "They want her real personality hidden. They want her to be the Goddess. The minute you get rid of the cult and latch on to the people with the cameras and the sneakers, you're in. Now on the show, she's making like Dinah Shore, having a relationship with her guests. You have to sell what she is, basically a little girl. And you want to see a little girl have a wonderful time."

To appeal to the camera-and-sneaker clan, CBS sanctioned a "humanizing" of Miss Garland. "It is a subtle system of de-glamorizing her by pointing up her problems," Worth's partner, Sultan, explained. "We're just being honest." On camera, Garland now jokes about the double chins she used to have and her once-muddled finances. Instead of guests idolizing her, they say things on the air to denigrate her. The remarks are more often painful than funny. Guest star Steve Lawrence needled, "Judy, you used to be so fat," and, "Why weren't you at rehearsals all week?" "This isn't the original, this is the twelfth Judy Garland," resident comedian Jerry Van Dyke said on a recent show. "The original went over the rainbow years ago." Then he added: "There's a little farm in Pasadena that grows Judy Garlands."

Another Van Dyke gibe, repeated in one form or another show after show, was, "What's a nice little old lady like you doing on television?" For a surefire laugh, Van Dyke would ask her to sing *Over the Rainbow*.

Van Dyke walked out

"On the first couple of shows she was on a pedestal," Hunt Stromberg explains. "Now in a lighthearted way, we are debunking this glamour. She's one of the gang." Van Dyke, however, is not. He requested and received his walking papers after 10 shows, sensing the futility of his role. "My whole personality is a likable, bumbling, cornhusking guy from the Midwest," Van Dyke says. "They changed my character into a pressing, forward, aggressive person. They took me and turned me completely around. If the stuff I was saying was hilarious, I'd say OK. But the lines were bombing."

Judy was not shaken by the efforts to take her off her pedestal ("I don't know what humanizing or de-glamorizing is—I don't think I'm too glamorous or inhuman," she says), but evidently, she was shaken by the departure of Van Dyke. "I'm going to pretend it's just not happening," she told him. "I don't even want to talk about it. If I don't talk about it I won't think about it."

The absurd notion of debasing Judy's reputation as a legendary figure and molding her show into an imitation of other prosaic variety shows has been a disaster where it hurts most, in the audience rating polls. On the first national Nielsen survey Judy was soundly thrashed by the long-running NBC hit, *Bonanza*. "I don't believe in ratings," said Jewison, sipping from an orange coffee cup decorated with the words FEARLESS LEADER. "Ratings are a false yardstick. They're for the birds."

Yet under Jewison's stewardship the Garland show seems to have deliberately tried to bolster its ratings by hiring guest stars familiar to the at-home audience. The motives behind the signing of old reliables like Jack Carter, Steve Allen, Steve Lawrence and Vic Damone were plainly commercial. "I don't like to use the word *commercial*," says Stromberg. "It's an attempt to make the show more popular."

As if Judy didn't have enough troubles onstage, her marriage to Sid Luft, the ex-test-pilot-turned-manager, has complicated her life in off-hours. Married 11 years and separated three times, the Lufts recently have undergone a series of stormy squabbles. "Every time she has a thing with Sid," says a Garland associate, "it's obvious she's been upset."

Recently Judy has been forced to face a new series of unsettling developments. Director Bill Hobin decided he had enough of the frequent policy alterations, changed his mind about living in California, sold his show horse and resigned after completing the first 13 shows. Executive producer Jewison, $100,000 richer, left after heading up eight shows to direct a Doris Day film. "I'm too old for weekly television," said the 36-year-old Jewison. The CBS unit publicist assigned to the show was fired and a new brace of choreographers signed on. And a third set of writers replaced Sultan and Worth, who withdrew to work on another show.

Lately, Judy's advisers have backed down from what was once an aloof attitude toward the press. Judy has submitted to dozens of interviews with TV editors in an obvious bid to attract new viewers through widespread publicity.

CBS official Stromberg, however, denies all the distress signals. "Not in any way, shape or form is this show in trouble," he steadfastly maintains. Judy herself is not quite so uncritical. "I would like to see the show become a little simpler," she says. "I don't think I'd like to look at my show every week. It's just enervating. I think it should be a bit easier for people to watch. We're in trouble unless we all calm down a bit."

The curious paradox in the TV troubles of Judy Garland is that everybody associated with her, both past and present, speaks of the singer only in the most reverent terms. "The time I spent with Garland I had such a ball, I wouldn't give that time up for anything in the world," says George Schlatter, who was later hired by NBC for two specials. "As far as Judy herself is concerned, I love her," says Hobin, now producing and directing a Victor Borge special for ABC.

"Judy is a legend in her own time," says Jewison. "She is a combination of Sammy Davis Jr., Aimee Semple McPherson and Greta Garbo." Unfortunately, both he and CBS tried to transform her into a composite of Garry Moore, Perry Como and Dinah Shore. They failed to realize there was nothing wrong with the old, the genuine Judy Garland.

Legend and Lies

Judy described how she and Mickey Rooney were worked beyond endurance making *Babes in Arms* in 1939: "They'd give us pep-up pills to keep us on our feet long after we were exhausted. Then they'd take us to the studio hospital and knock us cold with sleeping pills. After four hours they'd wake us and give us pep pills so we could work another seventy-two hours." The story is untrue. Yet it, and others similarly cruel, have found their way into every biography of her. These were tales told by Judy Garland, teller of tales; and in the years since her death, they have been repeated, refurbished and retold.

—Garland biographer Gerold Frank to the *Ladies' Home Journal*
1975

Comer Clarke

FROM *TITBITS*   OCTOBER 23, 1965

Judy Garland: "I've Been a Fool"

Comer Clarke has met the biggest stars in show business and been in on their most intimate conversations. He traveled more than 10,000 miles to meet them in their homes, on studio sets and backstage.

They confessed all—their secrets, fears, ambitions—exclusively for TITBITS.

Today Judy Garland tells how her daughter Liza saved her show business life . . . and Liza gives the secret behind her mother's flops.

It was two in the morning. The delirious, packed nightclub crowd sent wave after wave of cheers and applause surging across the floor. The beams of the spotlights spun again from their temporary resting place on the sweat-soaked band as the tiny, waif-like figure ran on the stage again and stood hands clasped and head bowed before the wildly excited crowd.

Then, in spontaneous unison, the audience rose to its feet in final, roaring tribute. Men threw roses from their button-holes and women wept. Judy Garland, her sad, wistful, blue eyes brimming, too, with tears, took a last bow and ran back to her dressing room.

It happened in California. But, after Judy's brilliant, flawless, one-and-a-half-hour performance, it would have happened anywhere.

Later, Judy Garland, a little tired but smiling joyfully, told me: "At last I've found my crock of happiness and contentment. You know there have been many times when I've been in despair."

Then she admitted: "I've been a fool in many ways. I've let my hopes, my feelings and my fears get on top of me so many times. I know I have sometimes put on a show that wasn't good enough. That I have let my emotions run away with me. I couldn't help it."

For a woman who became a dazzling Hollywood star while still in her teens, it was a bitter confession. But it was true.

To most people Judy Garland has been one of the most puzzling of Hollywood's great stars. Few of her millions of fans throughout the world have followed the breakdowns and emotional crises which have marred her career without a feeling of sadness and pity.

Her successes were golden from the moment she captivated the world as the wide-eyed, wondering girl in *The Wizard of Oz*.

Many other achievements followed. Then, somehow, the rocket climb faltered. Her crashes were as painfully public as her successes. And they became more and more frequent. Within the last couple of years the emotional crises appeared to have deepened.

Near-collapses and seeming *uncertainty* on stage . . . *fluffed* lines . . . *failure* to hit the right notes . . . *late* appearances . . . *inability* to finish acts . . . Judy's Australian tour last year seemed little short of disastrous.

Millions of British fans remember her performance in the TV show *Judy and Liza* from the London Palladium, when she several times failed to hit the correct notes and seemed to lean heavily on daughter, Liza Minnelli. But, at the end she received a standing ovation, for few stars are as warmly liked as Judy.

This year, in Cincinnati, Ohio, some of her audience became angry when she unexpectedly stopped during her act, announced a surprise intermission and later walked on stage with her doctor, explaining that she couldn't continue.

Another time she was rushed to hospital for observation and it was explained she was "emotionally upset" after "allergic reaction to a drug."

Brilliant

Eleven days after, at Las Vegas, oxygen was rushed to her hotel cottage when she became ill.

The incidents were only a few of many. Fans watched with sadness and sympathy. The once dazzling star was becoming one of the fastest falling-stars in show business. A brilliant meteorite burning out and streaking to oblivion.

In the dressing-room of that West Coast nightclub, I knew I was looking at a new Judy Garland. She said quietly and thoughtfully: "Yes, my daughter Liza and my two younger children saved me . . ."

She paused and then went on: "I suppose the song "Somewhere, Over the Rainbow" in *The Wizard of Oz* is what people most associate with me. But most people associate a rainbow with the fairytale crock of gold. I never sought for gold.

"What I have sought is what the little girl I portrayed in the film was searching for in that land over the rainbow—happiness, contentment and peace of mind. During these last few months, I seem to have found them."

She spoke these words with conviction. The change is immediately noticeable and close friends and casual acquaintances have noticed it, too.

What has happened in Judy Garland's life during the past few months to bring about this zestful happiness where, for so long, there seemed to be only bleak despair?

"I guess I've always been the nervous kind," Judy said. "And I guess I've often worried and been upset when I didn't have cause. But much of my trouble has been due to the fact that my marriages have failed.

"For myself, this need not have been too upsetting, although, naturally, I regretted it. But it's different when you have kids. At least, it ought to be different, I think. It certainly had an effect on me.

"I was divorced from my husband, Vincente Minnelli, when Liza—she's 19 now—was only six. I know how much a girl needs her mother as she grows up. I guess that, as the years passed, I worried more and more about her.

"In show business, you're away from home a lot. Film and singing commitments seemed to take me all over the world. But, as often as I could, I worked here on the West Coast—in Los Angeles, San Francisco or in nearby Las Vegas—so that I wouldn't be too far away.

"I know the effect broken homes have on kids, particularly if they think parents don't care. Specially a mother."

Then Judy Garland fell in love with Sid Luft and they got married.

"Everything was happy for a while and we had two children, Lorna, who's now 11 and Joseph, who's now nine," said Judy. "But, as a producer, Sid was away a lot and so was I.

"Sid and I drifted apart. Showbiz is rough on kids, I guess. But neither of us knew anything else and that's the way it went. I had to earn my living."

Tortured

"I used to spend hours awake, when I should have been sleeping, thinking about the unfairness of it all to those kids. I tortured myself over and over again by asking, 'Judy, did you do the right thing having them?'

"I had to take pills to make me sleep. If ever I overslept there were rumours that I'd taken an overdose.

"But I knew those kids needed a mother most of all, even though their parents had split up. I knew, too, that to gain custody, some dirty linen would be bound to be washed. Sure enough it was. The legal battles seemed endless."

Said Judy: "It all played on my mind. Every bit of tittle-tattle was a big headline. I knew the children would know. If you're a 'name' there's nothing you can do about it.

"And, you know, when you're going through a bad time, there are always plenty of people ready to help push you further downhill. They try to 'murder' you with all sorts of wild rumours. The worst interpretation is put on everything.

"When I was way out there in front of the footlights I often used to be thinking of my kids—and fluff my lines. And sometimes I was so distraught I just couldn't go on.

"Stupid? Maybe. But I guess that's how I'm made—a worrier."

I knew what she meant. For, earlier, in New York, I had talked to her beautiful and talented daughter, Liza.

Crumpled

"I have the best mother in the world," she said. "If she has faults, they are that she is warm and human. And that doesn't do in show business. It's easier if you're tough and hard.

"A lot of people have hurt her a lot of times and because she's thin-skinned and has taken lots of knocks in life she's crumpled now and again. But, believe me, no children could have a kinder, more thoughtful mother."

Liza went on to tell me what she meant.

"One night, when I was studying in Paris, my mother phoned from Los Angeles after the first part of her show to see how I was. I think she guessed I was a bit 'down' and homesick. She's always really believed in that rainbow, you know, and that we all eventually find happiness.

"She said: 'You just go on believing, Liza.' And there and then started to sing me a lullaby she used to sing me when I was just a little girl. After a few minutes I went to sleep, still clutching the phone. That's what she means to me and that's the kind of woman she is.

"She was always scared I might be mixing with Left Bank drifters. Once, when I told her on the telephone that I was going out in a sweater and jeans, she sent a complete wardrobe out from the best shop in Los Angeles. With the clothes was a little note saying: 'Just keep the sweater and jeans for lounging about in the apartment, honey.'"

Worry

"I guess she spent thousands of dollars on phone calls. Yet, when we went on tour together, I realised how great the toll of worry had been.

"Yes," Liza went on, "everyone is saying she's a new person now. It's all so wonderful."

Liza said of Judy's just-announced intention to marry her actor friend, Mark Herron, 29: "I think it's so marvelous. They are devoted. And we *all* get on so well together. We'll be a family again."

Back in her dressing room, Judy Garland, a young-looking 41, told me the real truth about the return after so long of the self-confidence and happiness which had once seemed to have left her. She admitted, "Liza really saved me. Despite everything, despite the broken marriages and the upsets anxiety caused, she has grown into a self-confident young woman—a success in her own right and a fine actress.

"She says she's tougher than I am—and I'm glad. She says she doesn't want to be a great star—just to fulfill herself in life. That's what I lived and worked and worried to bring about for her and my two other children.

"I know," said Judy, "that every mother will understand what I mean. In these past couple of years, when everything seemed to be going wrong, it was Liza who was on hand. She used to say: 'Mother, you were there when I needed you.'"

Judy went on: "But, really, four wonderful things have happened within the last few months this year and they are all things which have taken away the doubts and anxieties which have caused so much trouble in the past."

Judy counted them out on her fingers . . .

"One, Liza is a success in her own right as the star of the Broadway show *Flora, the Red Menace*. D'you know, she's just won a Tony—the Antoinette Perry Award—as the best musical actress of the year. Isn't that good?

"Two, after so much legal back and forth, I'm finally divorced from my former husband, Sid Luft. I have always felt it better to cut completely if two people don't get on.

"Three, I now have a full legal share of the custody of our two children, Lorna and Joseph. Sid had long fought for sole custody. I was scared to death I was going to lose them.

"Four, I'm going to marry Mark—Mark Herron. My three children adore him. So, at last, everything is wonderful all the way."

Judy Garland sat back in her chair and smiled.

"Now I have so much to live for," she said. "All those past problems are settled and the children of my marriages are growing up good and straight. I'm content."

I said goodbye and slipped out of the door as a messenger brought in another bouquet of flowers. It really seemed that Judy Garland has, at last, found that long-elusive happiness that has lain all these painful last few years on the other side of her rainbow.

The Plot Against Judy Garland

I am never going to eat lunch again. Never.

Bad things seem to happen to me at lunch. Years ago, when I was fired by Metro-Goldwyn-Mayer, I was fired at lunch; I always wondered why. And this past April, an odd thing happened to me while I was having lunch at the 20th Century–Fox studio in Hollywood, where I was making *Valley of the Dolls.*

I got fired again. Oh, I know the studio says I "withdrew for personal reasons," but don't believe a word of it. Judy Garland was fired, canned. Why, I don't know.

There I was eating lunch in my dressing room—and not feeling particularly well. I'd been fighting a flu bug all week long, and I had a low grade fever to prove it: just ask my doctor. Even so, I had reported to the set on time every day. And I had been working smoothly and hard. Nobody had complained that I wasn't. I had recorded the song I was to sing in the picture, and they all said it was great. I was delighted with my wardrobe—and with the nice salary I was earning: $100,000.

Then into my dressing room walked Owen McLean, talent executive under young Richard D. Zanuck, who now runs 20th Century–Fox. With him came a studio attorney.

"We're tired of your foolishness," McLean said. "We're just not going to put up with it anymore."

"What foolishness?" I asked. I wondered what in heaven this man was talking about.

He looked at me as if I were a child. "We can't use you," he said. "You're through. And you're not going to get a cent."

I was stunned. "Would you please repeat that slowly?" I asked.

He did. I had signed a contract. I was doing a good job. But I was still o-u-t.

Before long the nasty rumors began to drift around again: "Judy Garland blew another big chance."

Blew another big chance? I did not! I will not believe it till I hear just what the studio says I did, what terrible crimes I committed against their movie. Maybe young Zanuck wanted to show he was just as tough as his old man, Darryl. All right, they convinced me. It's just as well, though. I wanted the part, I needed the money, but I have to be honest: *Valley of the Dolls* isn't my kind of motion picture. I don't want to be a harridan on the screen, and I don't think people want me to be.

Actually, this latest setback isn't the end of the world for me. Things were a lot worse last year, when I literally didn't have a quarter and faced the possibility that the Internal Revenue Service would take away my house because I was behind on my tax payments. My car was repossessed and there were a few times when I wondered if I would be able to pay my grocery bills. I had no income whatsoever.

I've been in show business for 42½ years. I've earned about $10 million in salary and royalties from movies, television, concerts and recordings. And I've earned hundreds of millions of dollars more for the companies I worked for. But I've never lived like a wealthy woman because I've never been a wealthy woman. I never saw most of the money I earned. Never had a million dollars in the bank, or anything near that amount. At one time I was one of the greatest movie stars—with the most ragged underwear. I didn't have one petticoat that didn't have a rip in it.

I can live without money. But I find that I cannot live without love, without friends. And, until very recently, I have too often been a woman alone.

I don't approve of Arthur Miller as a person, because I don't think he understood Marilyn Monroe very well, but I do love his line from *Death of a Salesman:* "Care must be taken; attention must be paid." Miller was talking about his aging salesman, Willie Loman, but that's the way I feel about myself, too: "Care must be taken; attention must be paid."

*   *   *

One of the best friends I ever had was President John F. Kennedy. When I was doing my TV series, there were times when I didn't think I was getting the right advice. So I would telephone President Kennedy at the White House, and he would accept my calls.

It's funny, but the Los Angeles operators could never get used to my calling the White House, person-to-person. I'd ask for the President, or his secretary, Mrs. Evelyn Lincoln, and I could hear the operator tell another that "Judy Garland has flipped again—she thinks Lincoln is still in the White House!"

I remember that Mr. Kennedy was in a meeting when I called one evening, but he came right on the phone anyway.

"Hi theah," he said. "How's the television show going?"

I told him I had some problems, but I said that I knew he was busy and I certainly didn't want to take up his time. He said, "That's not important. You're just as important to me as the meeting. We love your show, and we've changed the White House dinner hour on Sundays so we can watch you. Now what's the matter?"

I told him, "Norman Jewison is coming in to direct the show for xxx a week, and I don't think I can afford him."

"Do you want Jewison?" the President asked.

"I don't mind him," I replied, adding that it was CBS's expensive idea.

"Well, then," Mr. Kennedy said. "CBS should pay him—and they will. You see to it that they do. Don't you put out one cent."

When I told him I would try to follow his advice, he said: "All right, now sing me the last eight bars of 'Over the Rainbow.' Make my day a little easier."

So I sang for him, by long-distance: ". . . if happy little bluebirds fly . . . beyond the rainbow . . . why, oh why, can't I?"

I knew Marilyn Monroe and loved her dearly. She asked me for help. Me! I didn't know what to tell her. One night, at a party at Clifton Webb's house, Marilyn followed me from room to room. "I don't want to get too far away from you," she said. "I'm scared!"

I told her, "We're all scared. I'm scared, too."

"If we could just talk," she said. "I know you'd understand."

I said, "Maybe I would. If you're scared, call me and come on over. We'll talk about it."

That beautiful girl was frightened of aloneness—the same thing I've been afraid of. Like me, she was just trying to do her job—to garnish some delightful whipped cream onto some people's lives. But Marilyn and I never got a chance to talk. I had to leave for England, and I never saw that sweet, dear girl again. I wish I had been able to talk to her the night she died.

I don't think Marilyn really meant to harm herself. It was partly because she had too many pills available, then was deserted by her friends. You shouldn't be told you're completely irresponsible and be left alone with too much medication. It's too easy to forget. You take a couple of sleeping pills, and you wake up in 20 minutes and forget you've taken them. So you take a couple more, and the next thing you know you've taken too many. It's happened to all of us; it happened to me. Luckily, somebody found me and saved my life.

There have been times when I have deliberately tried to take my life. Once I tried to cut my throat with a razor blade. But I don't think I really wanted to die, or I would have. I think I must have been crying for some attention. You see, I really like life. I am too stubborn to kill myself. My God, I've got too much to live for. I've got my children, maybe some grandchildren soon, and committing suicide would mean robbing too many people, including myself.

I think that what pulled me through my crises in the old days were friends. Marilyn Monroe needed some friends like I had—Errol Flynn, Humphrey Bogart and John Wayne. Bogart used to tell me, "You're OK, kid. Don't worry." And Errol told me all the time, "You'll be all right, Judy. The rest of us will go, but not you. You're the only one who'll always be all right." John Wayne was raised in Lancaster, Calif., where I grew up. He told me, "If you can live through Lancaster, Judy, you can live through anything." He's right.

Where are my friends now? I have few that I didn't pay for, and when the money ran out, they ran out, too. My fair-weather friends float out of my life when I'm in trouble. But most of them came into my life wearing parachutes anyway: then they bail out and leave me without a chute.

There have been good people in my life, of course. One year, when my state income taxes hadn't been paid, I was put in jail. I called people to bail me out. But you know who wound up helping me? Peter Lawford. He's one of the nicest men in the world. Roddy McDowall is a fine friend. So are Kay Thompson, George Cukor, Myrna Loy and Mickey Rooney. Since we were children, Mickey and I have tried to help one another. But we were always stopped or interfered with by intermediaries. We still do cling together in many ways. And during World War II, Dirk Bogarde was a British soldier serving in Burma. He was lying in the jungle rain one night and heard Japanese soldiers playing one of my records, "Look for the Silver Lining." When Dirk's group captured the Japanese, he took the record—and still has it on his wall. He's a dear man.

The nights have been especially bad for me. A man can always hire a girl. But a lady can't do things like that. I can't just pick up a man and become his lover. I'd like to have the ability to handle men and be a swinger, but I really don't know how.

Certainly I've had love affairs in my life. And they were wonderful because I *was* in love. With Tyrone Power, for instance. We were going to be married. Then World War II came along and somebody in Hollywood convinced me that I'd really fallen in love not with Tyrone but with the cover of *Photoplay*. He talked me out of waiting for Tyrone to come back from the war.

There's nothing worse than being home alone at night—and I have been, too often. There's too much of a gulf between the roar and the love of an audience I've entertained and the silence of my room. I can't stand the silence. I feel as if I hadn't been born. There seems to be no in-between for me. And I don't know how to cope with those empty nights. I know I'd rather have a few words of love at night than the approval of thousands of people.

Would you believe there have been times when I haven't even been asked out—not even to a movie! I've looked at the telephone many a night, and thought that if somebody would just get the wrong number I'd appreciate it. Just to hear the phone ring. Often I've tried to walk off the loneliness, just pacing the floor. I've had mass love—and that's pretty good, I guess—but not individual love, and that's so much better.

When I can't pace the floor anymore, I read. I read my old newspaper clippings, believe it or not. Or I turn on records of my Carnegie Hall concerts—that's what Rock Hudson and Marlon Brando tell me to do. They're wonderful men. You call them, and they'll drop whatever they're doing to help you. Donald O'Connor, whom I've known since he was a baby, is the same way.

Katharine Hepburn and Spencer Tracy tried to take care and pay attention. The last time I saw Kate Hepburn I was very ill in bed, with reporters and photographers outside my house. But I heard this flivver that she always drives wheel into the yard, and I thought, Oh, golly, here comes Hepburn health. Then I heard a great deal of commotion. Kate was carrying a heavy, shoulder-strap handbag, and she just beat her way through the press. She came into my bedroom and said, "Oh, dear, dear, you really are sick. I think you'd better come and stay at my house for a few weeks"—where she could throw me in the pool seven times a day, rush me around the block and put me through daily health exercises. But actually she had to start a movie the next day and couldn't take care of me. Finally, she went out the back door, climbed over a high fence and hiked all eighteen holes of the Los Angeles golf course to avoid the reporters out front. When she got to the clubhouse, she had someone bring her car to her.

I hadn't seen Spencer Tracy for a long time when he died last June, not since we made *Judgment at Nuremberg* in 1961. But during that picture, he threatened to punch another actor in the nose if he didn't read his lines correctly for me. I'll never forget Spencer saying to this man: "You S.O.B., if you continue to do this in front of me, to a woman I consider a famous actress, I'll kill you."

Bette Davis is a good friend, although we don't see much of each other now; she has a life of her own to lead. The last time I met Bette was in New York. She saw me with my fourth husband, Mark Herron, and immediately embarked on a tirade about how horrible men are. Mark almost fainted.

Recently, when the income-tax people were about to take my house away, I got help from another old friend, Senator George Murphy. He's a Republican and I'm a Democrat, but that didn't matter. George interceded with the government in my behalf; he told them it was unnecessary and humiliating for them to seize my home. He found time to take care of me as a person. The government held off, and now my tax situation has been worked out satisfactorily. I've since sold the house for $130,000.

Just as my recent troubles have taught me who my friends are, so, too, have I begun to discover my enemies. Some of them were pretty close to home. I seem to attract people who want to destroy me in order to stay alive. If you're a walking, living legend, some people just seem to want to hack away at it. It's never women who do it; just the men. They think of me just as a commodity, and want to prove that they can control me. If I get hurt in the process, that's too bad.

Four years ago, for example, I was riding the crest of a Judy Garland boom. I'd just done 42 concerts in 42 towns in 42 nights, and was in the midst of taping my 26 television shows. That tour must have grossed more than $1 million and paid off all the debts I had run up—with a little left over for me.

In addition, the television show paid $150,000 per week. Out of that, Kingsrow Productions, my company, had to pay for everything—guests, costuming, sets, the crews and the people in the booth, makeup people and all the rest. After I got through paying, there was no money left for me. No income at all.

Actually, during the TV taping I had begun to realize that too much money was being spent foolishly. I don't even know if I drew a regular salary. I checked the bank statements all the time, and it looked as if some of the accounts were gradually growing.

Then, suddenly, during a two-month period, I noticed a decline in the money I had accumulated. I realized that funds had been attached for bills that had not been paid. I was in trouble.

It would have helped if I had been a very dumb girl. Actually, people treated me as if I didn't have a brain in my head.

Once, one of my hangers-on rushed up and told me that a newspaper had taken a picture of me nude, and was going to publish it. My "friend" said that out of his own funds he had paid a large sum of money for the negative. Now he wanted me to pay him back.

I couldn't believe that any such nude picture existed. But since a man I trusted insisted that it did, and that he'd paid a lot of money for it to protect me, I said all right and paid him. But it's odd, I never saw the negative; neither did he, I'm sure. That money probably went to pay off some of his gambling debts.

In May of 1965, to clear up some of my financial problems, I was sent off on a tour of Australia. An entourage of 26 people went with me, some of them absolute strangers. I made three appearances in Australia—two in Sydney, one in Melbourne. I didn't know that Sydney and Melbourne are like Los Angeles and San Francisco; If you're a success in Sydney, you've got to be killed in Melbourne. And vice versa. I just went and tried to sing. Sydney was a tremendous success. But the Melbourne crowds were brutish, and so was the press.

At my hotel in Melbourne, the press bored holes through the walls to spy on me. They'd taken the suite next to my bathroom and bedroom. So I went around with Q-Tips and stuck them through the holes. I heard screams on the other end where I'd jab the peeper in the eye. I think that is one of the reasons the reporters got mad at me.

In June of 1965, after the Australian disaster, I went to Hong Kong for a rest. Instead I had a heart attack and a complete physical collapse from overwork. So I took two months off and traveled around the world. I needed the rest although I did make one appearance with my daughter, Liza Minnelli, at the London Palladium. I still didn't know I was in financial trouble, but I sensed that I would have to go back to work soon to put something into the kitty.

By spring of 1966, I realized how serious my financial difficulties were. I was advised that I might have to file for bankruptcy. But I refused to do it. I couldn't understand how I could have spent so much money.

Meanwhile, my life had become even more complicated by a man. On November 11, 1965, after my divorce from my third husband, Sid Luft, became final, I married Mark Herron. Mark had come into my house one Sunday night with a party of people. And he just didn't leave. He came back the next weekend and the weekend after that. Everybody else would leave, but he would still be around. So I said to myself, I guess he's OK. He just walked into my life like most people have as if I'm some kind of terminal. Like Grand Central Station—people just walk in and out, or right straight through. Some stay around until the building closes.

After I married Mark, I practically couldn't find him. He actually left right after the wedding ceremony; he said he had to be back in Los Angeles to work with some little theater group. It hadn't been too bad to fight with Sid Luft. He could fight back. But I never knew where Mark was. I used to hear from him once in a while. I think he called from a phone booth on casters.

How could I let all this happen to me? Well, for one thing, I'm not very tough. I've always dealt almost exclusively with men. And if you're completely feminine and you're dealing with big businessmen, you can't walk in and say, "Look, you're nothing. You don't know anything. You're bums, no-talents. I'm the star. You sit down and listen to me." That sounds like Helen Lawson, the tough, musical-comedy-star-on-the-skids I was supposed to play in *Valley of the Dolls*. But it's not Judy Garland. I'm a lady. I can't castrate men, so I let them maintain their egos while they robbed me of my vanity. If you ruin a man's ego, you rob him of his ability to do his job. I don't know how to fight like a man. I'm not supposed to know how. Still I must have some kind of toughness just to stay alive—a resilience.

When I review my financial problems, I have to admit they began with my mother. Mother was the worst—the real-life wicked witch of the West.

She had a marvelous talent for mishandling money—mine. When I was put under stock contract at Metro and had a steady income for the first time, we lived in a four-unit apartment building. I suggested to Mother that we buy it as an investment and rent the other three apartments. She hit me in the mouth and invested the money in a nickel mine in Needles, Calif., that has never been found. We never got a nickel back.

Actually, Mother was no good for anything except to create chaos and fear. She didn't like me because of my talent. She resented it because she could only play "Kitty on the Keys" like she was wearing boxing gloves. And when she sang, she had a crude voice. My sisters had lousy voices, too. My father had a pretty good voice, but he wasn't allowed to talk.

Sometimes it seems as if I've been in bondage since I was a fetus. Actually, I was put on the stage 2½ years after I was born. I enjoyed it because, while I didn't get any affection from my family, I got applause from strangers. George Jessel gave me my last name, Garland, and I thought of the first name, Judy. Then I became a thing instead of a person. And I never wanted to be that. I just wanted to be Frances Ethel Gumm, lady with a heart.

If it wasn't my mother or the studio, then it was my husbands. There's hardly been a time when I wasn't married, but while I was married to four men, I hardly met any of them. David Rose, my first husband, was too busy with his little toy trains. Vincente Minnelli, my second, was too busy for me. Sid Luft, my third, was in the charm business then. But Sid has been sweet lately. He doesn't want anything of me now, except my happiness, and he's been acting as my manager again. He's been instrumental in helping me settle my financial problems and in planning my future career. We're good friends.

Of course, I've done some dreadful things to my husbands. Vincente Minnelli snored louder and longer than any man in the world. After two years of this I was going crazy. We only had one bedroom, so there was no getting away from it. One night I sat up in bed and hit him as hard as I could with my fist—the one on which I wore my heavy wedding and engagement rings. I broke the poor man's nose. He woke up yelling and holding a horribly bloody nose. I quickly took some of the blood and smeared it on his night table and convinced him he had thrown himself against it during a nightmare.

It didn't cure Vincente's snoring, but he did build another wing on the house so I could sleep in peace.

Fortunately the current crisis in my life hasn't affected my children—Lorna and Joey Luft. Lorna is 14 and Joey is 12; they've seen me go through absolute hell, and they've gone through it with me—which has just made us laugh and love a little harder. They're proud that their mother is Judy Garland. But then I've finally gotten to the point of being proud of being Judy Garland, too.

Last year Lorna played a part on TV. When her income-tax refund came in the spring, $172, she knew that I needed money. She offered her $172 to me. Imagine that! I took it—she wanted to help, and would have been hurt if I hadn't—and two weeks later I used the money to buy her new dresses.

I've heard how "difficult" it is to be with Judy Garland. Do you know how difficult it is to *be* Judy Garland? And for *me* to live with me? I've had to do it—and what more unkind life can you think of than the one I've lived?

I'm told I'm a legend. Fine. But I don't know what that means. I certainly didn't ask to be a legend. I was totally unprepared for it.

Honest to God, I'd have been better off if I'd gone to school like other girls, attended the proms, and married some nice man. I've been a successful commodity for almost 43 years, but I apparently have yet to prove I'm a successful person—except to myself, in my own gut. But for now, it's enough that I feel better and am sleeping better than I ever have. I can get a whole night's sleep for the first time in 46 years. I'm sure I can still get some of the things I want: like a husband who loves me and would be with me every night. What more can a woman want?

I got my divorce from Mark Herron last spring, which freed me to marry Tom Green, whom I met 2½ years ago and with whom I have been in love for the last year and a half. I know what you're thinking. I'm 45 and Tom is 29. But it really doesn't make any difference to us. Actually, I think Tom is ageless—he's much older than I am: at least he knows a lot more than I do. This is the first time I've known what real happiness is. The other times I have been pushed into marriage. But not this time. Tom is in love with me, not the star Judy Garland. My children love him, and he loves them. We will be married this fall in the chapel of his college, Dartmouth. I've already met his parents.

I've been told that I represent people's dreams. I'm grateful, but if I represent people's dreams, then I represent a lot more than I really am.

Please, all I am is Judy Garland—and I am tired of trying to behave like

Judy Garland is supposed to behave, tired of being considered a sinking legend that's still afloat but not worth bothering about. I don't think many people could have lived through what I have. I'm glad I'm a woman with enough guts to cry about the lonely, dead-end streets of her life, but still a woman with a dream in her throat.

What it amounts to, really, is that I've been a little girl who hasn't quite known where she was going. But now, at last, I know. Finished? Why, I'm right at the beginning of something.

Judy on Judy

"Isn't it remarkable that with all the horror, with all that I've been through, I never drifted into booze or pills?"

—Judy to ghostwriter Sanford Dody, 1967

IV Myth

Rick McKay

MAY 1996

Raised on Judy, or, What Chance Did a Boy Have?

What can I say? I love Judy Garland. I always have. But, then again, I didn't have much choice—I was raised on her. My mother served Judy for breakfast, lunch and dinner. Now, that couldn't have had anything to do with me growing up to be a gay man . . . could it?

Judy has always been a gay icon. The old expression "friend of Dorothy" was code for being gay years ago; it's making a comeback, I hear. But, of course, I didn't have a clue about any of this when I was a kid, getting my first Judy-infusions. When I found out, I was shocked. As a child, I had thought everybody loved Judy. Then I went to school and found out most kids didn't even know who she was! If they knew her at all, it was as Dorothy in *The Wizard of Oz*. That wasn't my Judy. My Judy was the '60s Judy: The tight, hyper, funny, little titan who sang her heart out on Sunday nights opposite "Bonanza" . . . which my father would rather have been watching. He didn't stand a chance in our family.

It was my mother who got me started watching Judy. She would get us all to bed, then stay up late by herself, smoking cigarettes, sitting at the kitchen table and watching splashy MGM musicals on the old black-and-white portable that sat on the Formica countertop. My bedroom was right next door. I couldn't stand to hear the hum of that TV and know I was missing something. No VCRs back then, remember? If I asked the right questions about the movies and players, she would let me stay up. That was

how my nocturnal love for movies and Judy Garland began—among other things. I should have known something was up when I saw Mickey in the swimming pool scene in *Love Finds Andy Hardy* and thought: "Who knew that Judy's friend had such a great body?" That should have been a clue.

I really did think life was like the movies. I knew Hollywood would be just like *A Star is Born* and that there was a handsome, tortured James Mason–like star in California, just waiting for me to sober him up . . . while I became a big, fat star myself. What did we know about co-dependency back then? Big, fat—in Hollywood, I wouldn't have to worry about my plump adolescence; that weight would fall right off. Look at Judy in *Summer Stock*. Twenty pounds overweight the whole movie, and it all miraculously disappears just in time to sing "Get Happy" wearing nothing but a tailored tux jacket, a fedora and an armful of handsome men. See? And in *I Could Go on Singing,* there she was—drunk, falling down, spraining ankles, losing her voice *and* her illegitimate child—and still she stumbled out on stage at the London Palladium and sang like a trouper. Who knew she was mouthing the songs to pre-recorded tracks? Who cared? It was all real, it had to be. Reality was either the Judy movies or my hum-drum life in Beech Grove, Indiana. What question was there?

These days, the rainbow that Judy made famous in *The Wizard of Oz* has become a gay coat of arms, a crest for a disenfranchised family all over the world. Back in the '60s, Judy was hardly a role model for any minority. Not by a long shot. I think that is one of the things I liked best about her. She was in the news all the time and, believe me, it wasn't for her good deeds. Usually, she made the papers because she was in some kind of wild trouble.

I remember my dad—a true Frank Sinatra aficionado, and no great fan of Judy's—loved to come home from work, sit down at the dinner table and announce Judy's latest press-worthy trauma. "Hey, did you see your friend Judy in the paper today? She was drunk and slugged a stewardess on a TWA flight." Or, "I see Judy GAH-land is looking for someplace to live. They threw her out of her hotel for not paying her bill. I'd like to have a buck for every million *she's* made." My favorite was: "Did you see your friend Judy on television today? Her and her three kids all running for a plane—in their pajamas! Escaping from her latest husband. Nice way to bring up kids, huh?"

Yes! A great way to bring up kids! I would have loved to grow up like that: Sneaking out of New York City hotels in the middle of the night, running for airplanes in your pajamas. Judy made Auntie Mame look like the

Singing Nun. And this wasn't even Movie-Judy—this was real life! What did dad think, that Liza, Lorna and Joey wanted to grow up in Beech Grove? Well, they're welcome to my bunk bed.

My mother revved up Judy in the morning, with her vacuum cleaner, and played Judy albums all day. Remember those stereo consoles we all had? Big, giant things that housed nothing but a cheap turntable and two tinny speakers. Homeless people could live in them . . . and probably do. My mother liked the live albums best: Judy at Carnegie Hall, Judy at the Coconut Grove, Judy at the Palladium or the Palace or the supermarket . . . my mother didn't care. The vacuum noise drowned out my mother's singing voice just enough to make her believe she could sing *a la* Garland. If you could have heard her you would have known better. Eventually, everyone in the family—and there were eight kids in our Irish brood—was singing Judy songs. What chance did a boy have?

My older brother and I were fascinated by the patter on those live albums. We would lay in our bunk beds at night and trade Judy-*mots*. I didn't understand the half of it, but I memorized every word she said between songs anyway. We would turn it into a dialog, a competition. "Do you— d'you like a foggy day? I like a foggy day . . ." (I never knew exactly what that meant—we didn't have fog in Indiana. But it sounded very sophisticated.) Or, "Do you really want more? Aren't you tired or anything? Well we've only got one more. We'll—we'll have to do Chi-cah-goh . . ." Or my favorite: "We'll sing 'em all—we'll stay all NIGHT!" My father would walk by and snort, "You two sound like a couple of fruitcakes!" I am willing to wager that I was the only kid in the western hemisphere who never said: " 'night Mom, 'night Dad." It was always: "I love you all very much! Good night—God Bless!"

Of course, the two of us *could* have been the only straight men in America who grew up memorizing Judy Garland patter. . . .

Soon I was obsessed; I wanted every Judy album. I couldn't afford them—record albums were a whole $4.98 back then. But then I stumbled on to a great way to make money. A well-meaning relative gave me a Beatles album for Christmas. I, of course, immediately went to exchange it for a Judy album. When the store had no Judy albums in stock, they gave me the money back instead. Hmm. . . .

I began to get up very early on Saturday mornings and leave my parents a note, saying I was riding my bicycle to the Beech Grove Drug Store to read comics. In reality, I would ride to 9th Street and Grovewood Avenue and hide my bike in the woods. Then I would take the city bus to downtown Indianapolis, 15 miles away. The bus ride alone was considered daring in our circle. In the Big City, I would buy record albums on sale at Woolworth's, and return them at the big department stores where they were more expensive. That's right—they would give me *cash* back! Sometimes my profit would be a phenomenal $3 an album. I could hit three different department stores in one day and make enough for two Judy records. No one ever suspected me; hey, I was *9*. And my face was honest, if not my nature.

I guess I developed my value system and sense of reality in front of a television. If there were no Judy musicals or great old movies on, mom and the kids would hit the talk show circuit. Judy was a popular guest on all the shows, too. She was a crack wit and would tell wicked stories about growing up on the M-G-M lot with Mickey Rooney, Lana Turner and the gang. She would shock Jack Paar with catty impressions of Deanna Durbin, Marlene Dietrich and Elizabeth Taylor. It was the first time I had heard one celebrity trashing another on TV—and I loved it. Dish elevated to an art form.

Judy might show up drunk, or with an English accent . . . if she showed up at all. There were more than a few times we would tune in and Judy wouldn't. When she did, she might show up on Mike Douglas with a broom, sweeping the stage, or on Merv Griffin with sordid stories about Louis B. Mayer or her days in vaudeville. She hit all the shows. Talk shows like Johnny Carson or Joey Bishop. Variety shows like Ed Sullivan, Garry Moore, Sammy Davis, Jr. and The Hollywood Palace. You never knew what you would get—but, you knew it wouldn't be dull. I wonder if David Letterman would have any idea how to handle her. I doubt it. But I would love to have seen him try!

I was only 13 when Judy Garland died, but I felt like I had known her forever. More than anything, I wanted to go to her funeral. My older brother, the one who had memorized Judy-patter with me, actually did sneak out of Indiana with his best friend, determined to see Judy at Frank Campbell's Funeral Home. The last time she would play New York. I could *not* miss it and did everything I could to convince him to take me along. I threatened to tell our parents he was running away, or that he had drank up my Dad's scotch. I threatened the ultimate: I would destroy *THE* album— *The Garland Touch*, which was out of print. No luck. He left without me. He even convinced me to loan him my last $5 to help him get there. He promised to bring me a souvenir. Small consolation to a mourning, 13-year old Garlandophile.

All that weekend, I watched the news on television. I saw crowds on Madison Avenue waiting for a chance to say goodbye to their Esther Blodgett. I saw Liza, Lorna and Joey . . . James Mason and Kay Thompson . . . but no trace of my brother. When he finally came home, broke and tired, he admitted he had gotten no farther than nearby Chicago. When I demanded my $5 back, he gave me an album he had bought in Chicago instead . . . "worth a lot more than $5," he said. I still remember the silver cover with the stark maroon letters: *JUDY—LONDON—1969.*

It was a recording her fifth and final husband had made with a cheap little tape recorder at her last engagement in London. Liner notes by Rex Reed . . . they might just as well have been the Rosetta stone. This was definitely Judy live, liver than I had ever heard her. She had had more than a few drinks before going on and she probably wasn't at her best. But, the Judy-patter! At one point she slurred to a girl in the audience: "How old are you, darling?" "18," the young girl replied. "Nobody's 18 anymore," Judy retorted, sounding dead sober. At the time, I thought 18 was ancient.

All that summer, I played Judy albums. I joined the *Columbia Record Club* so I could order more of them through the mail. My brother was getting ready for college and was moving out, leaving Judy behind. I was set to begin high school, and it was a new start for me. I had never really "fit in" before, and this was my last chance. I made a conscious choice to leave Judy behind, too. By the time I had enrolled in Catholic High School, I was mourning what seemed more appropriate deaths. Jimi Hendrix. Janis Joplin. I started doing school plays, decorating floats, and collected cans for fund-raising drives. Inside, I knew that I was gay, but I blocked it out. Gay was not something you could be in an Indiana Catholic school in 1969. It was not an option . . . but drugs were. From Judy I moved on to rock and roll concerts and tripping out on acid. It was 1969. I rationalized that if Judy had lasted, she would be trying LSD, too.

Through the years Judy would pop back into my life unexpectedly. Living in Boston at age 19 or 20, searching for myself, I would drink too much and find myself playing the *Carnegie Hall* album, trying to explain the mystique to an uninitiated stranger. In New York at 25, starting to work in the theater and cabaret, I would enter Colony Records looking for an obscure piece of sheet music and instead find myself scouring the bins for bootlegs of *Judy in Holland* or *Judy at the Palace*. Judy was not fashionable; Liza, Halston and Studio 54 were happening. But I never really put Judy away.

Twenty-five years after her death, when the anniversary of the Stonewall Riots (which occurred on the day of Judy's funeral) were celebrated and the rainbow was made an official gay badge, I went to Central Park for the festivities. Liza spoke of "Mama." There were guys there so young they had no idea who Judy Garland was. Still, more than a few did. A tiny theater with an even smaller budget put on a new play called '*Judy at the Stonewall Inn*' where Judy came back from the dead and helped out a drag queen. There was even a bus trip "Garland Graveyard Tour" to Judy's final resting place. They would throw in Joan Crawford, too, if you paid in advance.

I had been doing a solo act for years, but never mentioned anything *too* personal in my one-man autobiographical show before. Later that same week, I was asked to do an AIDS benefit. And I decided it was time to start telling the real stories of my youth and how I got where I am. Agents, club owners, critics and friends had always told me to leave the "gay thing" out of my show. It was . . . unnecessary, they said. But it was too late. I—and the times—had come too far. This wasn't 1969 and it wasn't Beech Grove, Indiana. I was going to tell my story on stage, and how could I leave Judy or the truth out of it?

It was time to tell the world that I was "a friend of Dorothy." Hell, I was raised on that girl!

Ralph J. Gleason

FROM THE *SAN FRANCISCO EXAMINER*   SEPTEMBER 2, 1965

The Enigma of Judy Garland

The best illustration of the truth of Bob Dylan's line "there's no success like failure" is the audience reaction to Judy Garland, who opened at the Circle Star Theater Tuesday night.

Her audience loves her for her weakness, more for what she cannot or can no longer do than for what she can. As Miss Garland trembled on the brink of utter disaster all evening, they screamed and clapped and were delighted.

For the voice is almost totally gone and the performance itself, in terms of showmanship, bizarre. Only occasionally was she able to summon the strength to belt out one of the famous Judy Garland tones in the upper register, and when she dropped down to the husky lower tones, her voice sometimes failed altogether, becoming only a whisper. It was an exercise in illusion, comparable to the John Charles Thomas substitution of a hand motion for a high note which James M. Cain describes in one of his novels.

"Over the Rainbow," once her *tour de force,* is now a combination of pantomime and sing-along, with Miss Garland reciting in a quavering voice that sounds like a combination of Tallulah Bankhead laryngitis and Joe E. Lewis boozy baritone. The truth is the Emperor, or in this case I suppose, the Empress, has no clothes. What other performer could get away with forgetting what song she was singing, forgetting lyrics, and then leaving by the wrong exit and still have her faithful applaud her rapturously?

Psychologists and sociologists need to examine the Garland Syndrome more than they do the Beatle fans. Is it that her fans love to know the idol has feet of clay? Do they really love to hear her tell, as she did in a rambling anecdote, how, on her TV show, "June Allyson got kinda drunk but I didn't know it. I was kinda drunk myself"?

Do her fans sense in the lyrics to songs like "Just in Time" and "What Now My Love" the tragedy and frustration of Miss Garland's own life?

She sang the latter number half sitting and half lying on the stage, rather like a James Brown bit, begging Mark Herron ("my beloved Mark who I'm going to marry on the 19th and don't you forget it") to come out and sing it with her because he always insisted she sing it. And the dream world of the lyrics of "Over the Rainbow" seemed very, very real to her. In fact, her entire performance had a dream-like quality to it, as though she were sleep walking, a puppet in red stretch pants and a striped blouse, hung there on strings.

Discussion

And what would a psychologist make of her discussion of herself in the third person? "There are no wings [on the stage] here to hide in if I get nervous and neurotic like Judy Garland does." And she told us, in the June Allyson anecdote, how she was a big star in Hollywood. "Oh I was big, really big," she said earnestly.

I find all of this pitiful and sorrowful and somehow embarrassing, just as I find her painful efforts to recapture her vocal powers painful and pitiful and embarrassing. When she wrestled with the highs of "The Trolley Song" or "Zing Went the Strings of My Heart," the audience loved her. But they can only have been loving the symbol and the image of what she was, not what she is now.

There is, incidentally, a similarity between her fans and the Beatle moppets. The conventions of expressing the ecstasy are quite different, but the emotion is the same. She can do no wrong for those who are committed. The second part of poet Bob Dylan's line goes, "and failure's no success at all." That's how it is for the rest of us.

Charade

Miss Garland will stagger through this grotesque charade, if all goes well, nightly through Sunday. There are seats for all performances, the Circle Theater people admit. Rumors of a sell-out are grossly exaggerated.

The first half of the show is a triumph of the sort of mediocrity the American middle class audience seemed determined to accept. The Steiner Brothers, who look like characters in "The Untouchables," do tap dancing and vocals and humor. The Young Folk, a group of seven singers who all look like Dick Clark except that some of them may be girls, provide a 20 minute interlude of fraternity house folk singing and high school life-of-the-party imitations. They are abominable. Charlie Manna, the comedian, is on for 25 minutes, for three giggles and a lot of applause for a routine that is like a real life version of Lenny Bruce's "Comic at the Palladium" bit. His jokes run the gamut from double entendre to sick.

The Garland opening performance took place a few hours after the Beatles' matinee at the Cow Palace, which I also attended. I would like to state publicly that I found the Beatles better singers, better showmen and the whole affair a lot more fun and a lot less sick than the Garland show.

Burt Korall

FROM *THE SATURDAY REVIEW*   SEPTEMBER 30, 1967

The Garland Phenomenon

The Judy Garland phenomenon was born and initially nourished in *The Wizard of Oz*, an M-G-M musical fantasy released in 1939. As Dorothy, the wide-eyed innocent, Miss Garland touched audiences deeply. She was good and believing, wholesome and vulnerable, determined and cheerful—a fulfillment of the Girl Scout oath.

Once the studio realized the impact the girl had made, the die was cast. Her image became fixed. Until the conclusion of her M-G-M affiliation in 1950, she played paragons of virtue. Graciously childlike, always seeking to please, she smiled bravely in the face of adversity, cried glycerin tears, or bubbled over with candy-cane happiness. Lavish, beautifully mounted musicals were her medium. Through a series of them, all structured to make audiences forget daily cares and sing and pretend along with the cast, Miss Garland sang vibrantly or with built-in sadness. She was a plastic figure who could sing about *real* emotions.

Young people, who did not grow up with the M-G-M Garland, also have an uncommon rapport with her. Their basis for it seems far healthier and in tune with the truths of life. They find in her live and recorded performances an honesty, a sense of fallibility, humanity, and loss very much at odds with her "Goody Two-Shoes" film image. They accept the lady for what she really is— a *person,* with her own unique set of problems. They sense her need for communion and a stabilizing hand, and a dialogue has been established.

141

Judy Garland is one thing to the older generation, another to the young. To both she represents an extension of themselves. In the United States or abroad, her fans present a united front. A Garland theater or concert engagement brings them out in force. For the "objective" observer, their ritual devotion is almost embarrassing in its intensity. They throw flowers, clap enthusiastically—seemingly on cue—laugh loudly, cry boldly, try to touch her.

The love is mutual. Garland *needs* them. She makes declarations of affection to her audience at crucial times during every performance. She draws people to her, gripping them tightly, as a frightened little girl would her mother's skirt in a tense situation. By the close of a Garland evening, feeling has built to crescendo force. In the final confrontation between Garland and audience, the dam bursts and a surge of affection engulfs the artist.

That Judy Garland is an entertainer has become secondary to the "event." Because of the fanatical response to a Garland performance, one can easily be swept along by the momentum basic to the situation. It is a temptation to ignore the performance and become immersed in the atmosphere. You must remove yourself from the center of the storm to sort things out. A recording allows this isolation.

This past August, Miss Garland, again on the comeback trail, played an enormously successful month's engagement with her two children at the Palace Theater on Broadway. A "live" ABC recording was one of the by-products of the stand. Titled *Judy Garland at Home at the Palace—Opening Night (ABCS-620),* it contains many of her big songs vividly arranged and well-played by a large orchestra directed by Bobby Cole. Most important, it reveals Garland as she is today.

Immediately apparent is one fact: the Garland voice is unstable. A tightrope walker in the voice's lower register, she must tread lightly in this area for fear of falling out of tune. Often her famed vibrato moves out of control. Where once there was smoothness, now there is strain. Fortunately, her middle-register work is a bit more stable and the big, belting notes are met head on and realized.

Garland has turned into an off-again, on-again singer who uses every device at her command to give a song interpretative strength. More often than not, she makes it. But some of her efforts in the album, particularly Schwartz and Dietz's "That's Entertainment," are shattering failures. These are the realities, above and beyond the clamor of testimony to her continuing popularity.

As you repeatedly listen to this album, however, a strange thing happens: the ragged voice and forgotten lyrics become progressively less important. For all the technical insufficiencies of the performances, she still gets across. Like an aging fast-ball pitcher, Judy Garland makes her experience and know-how pay. One has only to turn to her affecting reading of Cole Porter's comment on the chance aspect of life and love, "I Loved Him, But He Didn't Love Me," to realize her strength.

Hard, cold evaluation of a fading voice is easy. To go below the top layer of a performance is another matter. The sharpness and excitement of youth may be gone from Miss Garland's efforts, but the intrinsic spark remains. If you involve yourself with her for a little while, you *really* hear her and discover the artistic justification for the continuing phenomenon.

Headlines

Garland-Rose Divorce Final—June 1945

Director Minnelli to Wed Judy Garland—June 1945

Judy Garland and Mate Tell of Separation—March 1949

Garland Marries Actors Agent Sid Luft—June 1951

Judy Garland Files for Divorce: Charges Luft Beat Her—March 1958

Judy Garland Weds Mark Herron between Shows In Las Vegas—November 1965

Judy Garland Given Divorce from Herron: Charges He Beat Her—April 1967

Judy to Wed Again—December 1968

FROM *NEWSWEEK*   NOVEMBER 4, 1963

Question Mark

Judy Garland, 97 pounds of talented insecurity, sat in a CBS executive office one day last week—a fragile windmill dressed in gray. She gestured incessantly, crossed and uncrossed her thin legs, smiled sadly, and, looking somewhere over the rainbow, said: "For the first time in my life, I think, no, I'm sure I'm starting to like myself." That night, in her suite at New York's St. Regis Hotel, the 41-year-old star talked about one of the many problems besetting "The Judy Garland Show": Judy Garland's hands.

"I touch. I've always touched people. All the time I touched. It's a habit. It isn't nervousness. It's pure affection. I'm a woman who wants to reach out and take 40 million people in her arms, but I've been told [by CBS brass] that I must watch myself. I've also been told I shouldn't kiss my leading ladies on the cheek, that it offends some viewers. I've been a hit for years, and I always kissed and touched. But I'm the original take-orders girl. CBS knows more about television than I do. All they want for me is a smash."

Big Deal: Thus far, the Garland hour has been considerably less than that, running far behind its NBC competitor, "Bonanza," and fighting to outrate ABC's "Arrest and Trial." As a result, though only five shows have been screened (and six more taped), there have been shifts in producers, changes of writers, and the loss of a comedian, Jerry Van Dyke, a regular cast member who quit, under pressure. Since CBS has an $8.5 million investment in Miss Garland's first shot at weekly TV, more switches are planned. The show will pick up two new writers, a new director, and two alternating choreographers, Peter Gennaro and Carol Haney.

With the show already being dubbed "The Anatomy of a Headache," there was some serious huddling last week among the star and CBS's entertainment bosses: James T. Aubrey Jr., president of CBS-TV, and Mike Dann, vice president, programs. Aubrey had to fit his schedule to fit Judy's, and after one session that ended at 5:30 A.M., the CBS executive was at his desk four hours later, beat but confident that the Sunday-night program soon would be everything it could be. Miss Garland, who nets $30,000 per show, still seems less certain about its future course.

Rich Desire: "You just can't barge into people's living rooms and say I'm a big star," she said. "I like them to get to know me. And I'm not that experienced with so much taping. You get the feeling if you miss one word, you get shot. Maybe that's why I wanted so much to do the weekly series. For years everybody's been saying I couldn't do it, I couldn't stand the pressure every week. Now it's kind of like sticking my tongue out and saying: 'See, I'm doing it.' And I'm hoping someday to be very rich from this."

She ground out a filter-tip cigarette and lowered her eyes. "You know, I used to watch 'Bonanza' all the time, and if my show doesn't get better, I'll go back to watching 'Bonanza.' What do I think 'The Judy Garland Show' should be? Well, like my own life, really. Full of interesting personalities. But you have to listen to the network. We wouldn't get off the ground if we didn't, so we darn well better. If [CBS, Inc., president Frank] Stanton said dye your hair blond, I'd do it."

Because of Miss Garland's history of frequent emotional turmoil, CBS executives are keeping their fingers crossed. As one said: "Right now she is the biggest question mark for the whole '63–'64 season." Since the show's premiere, Miss Garland's singing has often been outstanding, but merely talking, even walking, she seems uncomfortable, and, on occasion, as she tugs at her ear or brushes her forehead, almost unnerved.

Mike Dann, an easygoing man whose office radio is usually tuned to the soothing music of WQXR, knows the most about what's going to happen in the show. He and Aubrey planned the changes, then passed them along to Miss Garland.

"We're trying to give Judy a program with a weekly thread to make her more acceptable in the heartland," Dann says. "In the second thirteen weeks we decided that she should never appear in sketches and never play any character but herself. And she'll be singing more medleys, more standards. Songs are her goodies. Her babies. We told her what we think, and she's listening. She's far too insecure about TV to exercise her own judgment. She knows we know what's good for her." And, ultimately, what's good for Judy Garland is good for CBS.

Judy Floats

At eleven-forty-three she began to let them touch her. They had been after her flesh a long while, but it is only now, after she is done and it is ended, that she allowed them contact. Just the barest graze. Her fingertips to theirs as she moved, as always jerkily, parallel to the footlights, right to left, then back. And if she expected her flesh to quiet them, she was only wrong: the din, already painful, went somehow up a notch, now almost completely covering the noise from the pit where the band went wearily on with "Over the Rainbow," over and over, "Over the Rainbow," over again. For this was August 26, Judy Garland's closing night at the Palace. And the hysteria had been a long time building.

By nine-thirty that night, when the first act of the show ended, the large outer lobby was already almost full. (There was no point to seeing the first act. Everybody knew that.) Now, as the lobby filled all the way, the audience itself began to become insistently noticeable. A stunning blonde walked by, in a lovely green jacket, sexy and confident and undulating with every step, and it comes as a genuine shock to realize the blonde is a boy. Two other boys flit by, chattering. First: "I got her pink roses and white carnations, you think she'll like it?" Second (*angry*): "Now why didn't I bring her flowers—oooh, it's just too late for me now." Another flutter of boys, half a dozen this time, and, watching it all from a corner, two heterosexual married couples. "These fags," the first man says. "It's like the concentra-

tion camps—some of them died along the way but a lot got here anyway." He turns to the other husband, shrugs, and adds, "Tonight, no one goes to the men's room."

But probably no more than a quarter of the house were obvious homosexuals. Two girls and a boy hurry through the lobby to their seats. "Wanna guess what I got her?" the first girl asks. "What—what?" from the second girl. "Would you believe a trunk of flowers?" "A *trunk*?" the boy says. "How you getting it on stage?" "I got a seat in the very front row," the first girl replies, homely but clearly triumphant.

By nine-fifty most of the audience is seated.

At nine-fifty-two there came the first burst of nervous applause, accompanied by the standard whispers preceding any Garland show: "Do you think . . . ?" "You don't suppose . . . ?" Rumor: Would she make it? Sure, she'll make it, she has to make it. I hear she's sick. No. She's fine. Well, if she's fine then where is she, it's almost ten and . . . "Judy!" someone shouts, and once the name is thrown there is a burst of applause, then suddenly another, louder burst as Liza Minnelli, Garland's daughter, takes her seat and everybody sighs with relief, because if the mother were sick, why would Liza be here?

Nine-fifty-seven and everyone on the main floor starts to turn around, staring at the rear of the house. Everyone knows she always makes her entrance from the rear of the house. Everyone knows that.

Ten and the lights dim. A minute later the conductor starts talking to the men in the pit and a minute after that: music. First the downbeat, then the drumroll and then a few notes of *The Man That Got Away* before the orchestra segues into *The Trolley Song,* and then another segue and it's *Over the Rainbow*. The audience is applauding the tunes. Of course they're applauding the tunes, why shouldn't they applaud the tunes, these are famous tunes, you'd expect the audience to applaud them, but what you wouldn't expect is that not only is the audience applauding all of the tunes, *tonight they're also applauding the segues.*

Ten-five and everybody stands up as if on signal, and the clapping and screaming, sporadic before, becomes concentrated, a force to be reckoned with. The screaming, unleashed, continues to build and build—she hasn't appeared yet, understand, no one's seen her—it's just that at ten-five on the button everybody began to scream and it didn't seem to matter that she wasn't there. The lady herself suddenly seemed almost superfluous, as if we all could have a terrific time standing there, shouting out loud, throwing kisses at the empty center aisle, and I kept thinking of the Indianapolis Clowns—I think it is—who play a few innings of baseball every so often without a ball, just miming the whole thing, and the crowds who come to see them love it as this crowd loved the empty center aisle of the Palace.

Then at ten-seven the aisle wasn't empty anymore. Because at the rear, she finally put in her appearance, and you know she isn't superfluous, because the old screaming, the pre-Garland screaming, that was nothing. Down the aisle she came slowly, slowly, throwing kisses to the people, mouthing, "Thank you, thank you," as the noise somehow grew, and along with the cries of "Judy!" came the words, "We love you, we love you!"

Ten-nine she reaches the stage and just stands there. The screaming is coming in waves now, and in a trough of quiet someone begs, "Never leave us," and with that the noise again, somehow, grew, and she still just stands there, holding a mike, the center of the world, and the noise can't get any louder, there is just no way, and perhaps she senses this because suddenly she is into *I Feel a Song Comin' On,* the hand mike close to her mouth, almost but not quite inside it. She stands there singing, legs spread wide and firm, her free arm jerking in the air, and somehow she seems mechanical, like Frank Gorshin's mimicking of Burt Lancaster.

And after the song and the screaming for it end, she moves into other songs, *Almost Like Being in Love* and *This Can't Be Love* and *Just in Time,* which is a mistake, it's bad for her, because the voice is incapable of holding a note any more and "just in time" goes "just in tiiiiimmmme" and she can't make it last, so she makes a sudden campy gesture and they love it and scream over it and by the time they are quiet again she's out of the song. Next a new song, and the audience doesn't seem to like it much, probably because it is new, and for the first time there is almost quiet in the house.

But not for long. Because pretty soon it's *The Trolley Song,* and at the very end of it there are the words "with his hand holding mine," and "mine" is a tough note, high and climactic, and as she gets to it she spreads her feet just a little wider and suddenly she's eating the mike—it's down her throat, jammed—and from somewhere she found it, because at precisely ten-thirty, on the word "mine," she hit the high note, all she had and on-the-button perfect and you could actually hear them gasp because she did it, she got a note right, a loud note yet, and she got it. It wasn't just that she was on pitch—she's almost always on pitch or at least you know she knows where pitch is if she's off it—it was pitch plus volume plus timbre plus whatever else it is that distinguishes one voice from another and this was Garland's voice, the old Garland's voice, back again, just like in the movies, and even though it was only for one note it was enough to tear the place apart.

There then followed half an hour of vamping. She did a dance and she introduced her daughter Lorna, who can't sing either, and then her son Joey did a few minutes of drum solos and then Liza came up and talked with her mother a while before singing, stunningly, *Cabaret,* and as Liza goes back to her seat Judy says, "Liza, you've been marvelous all your life and so have Liza and Joey," instead of "Lorna and Joey," maybe a Freudian slip, meaning Lorna wasn't good enough to be worth mentioning or Liza was so good it bugged her so she had to name her twice, or maybe it was just a standard slip of the tongue.

Now the bottom notes of *Old Man River* followed by *That's Entertainment* where she intentionally fluffs the lyric and the audience is clapping staccato now, and a middle-aged couple leaves and a young girl runs up to the stage and throws flowers to Judy, and that triggers it, because suddenly another girl is up there throwing flowers and then a man charges to the footlights carrying a wrapped box of something, and she's singing *Rock-a-Bye Your Baby With a Dixie Melody* as they begin closing in on the stage.

The aisles are filling, all of them, and now the trunk of flowers is pushed up from the front row, and it's not a big trunk, not a steamer trunk or anything like that, but it is a large box and it is full of flowers. And then a man of about forty pushes close and hands up a drawing he's made of her and cameras are everywhere and more girls with more flowers wedge in toward her and as the aisles pack tighter it's like Billy Graham at the end of his sell, standing on the dais, arms folded, going, "Y'all come now . . . come on . . . come on . . . we'll wait for you . . . Christ went to the cross for you, you can come this far for him, come on, come on, y'all come. . . ."

Eleven-thirty-two and *Swanee* and someone in the mass of the center aisle shouts *Over the Rainbow* and everybody whirls on him because part of the sacrament is that *Over the Rainbow* is the end, nothing after, ever, everybody knew that.

Over the Rainbow comes at eleven-thirty-four. She is sitting on the stage floor now, and just before the final "Why oh why can't I" she pauses long enough to shout: *"And I made it!"*—a ringing reply to all the unbelievers who thought she was finished.

And now, through the eleven minutes of curtain calls, more and more people press toward her. People sitting in the front rows who wanted to leave were trapped there. Curtain down and up. Curtain down and up. The clapping and the crying never die. And a young boy, maybe twenty-one, maybe less, is staring up at her and wringing his hands. He cannot and will not stop with his hands, even though his constant wringing pressure has forced the skin to burst. He holds a handkerchief as he continues to stare up at her and wring his hands and bleed.

And what is she to them that they should bleed for her? There are many generalizations that can be made about homosexuals, but here are two fairly obvious points. First, if they have an enemy, it is age. And Garland is youth, perennially, over the rainbow. And secondly, the lady has suffered. Homosexuals tend to identify with suffering. They are a persecuted group and they understand suffering. And so does Garland. She's been through the fire and lived—all the drinking and divorcing, all the pills and all the men, all the poundage come and gone—brothers and sisters, *she knows*.

The following from a screenwriter: "I don't understand the appeal, but I saw it work once, in this crazy way. I was at a party in Malibu—my first big Hollywood-type let's-all-get-slowly-smashed-on-Sunday party—and there were all these famous faces and I hid behind a Bloody Mary in the corner. There were a lot of actors there and the word on them was they were queer. But this was a boy-girl party, and everyone was paired off and all these beautiful men and gorgeous broads were talking and drinking like they were human after all.

"Anyway everything's going along and it's sunny and the beach is something and I'm getting a little buzzed in my corner position and this star-type female goes by me and I naturally look at her and she's wearing this fantastically loosely knit sweater—don't know what the hell it was but there wasn't a lot of it and also there's no bra and these famous breasts are bouncing by and I'd never seen any before, not famous ones, and they weren't much and I was thinking deep thoughts about that when I realized Garland was in the room. It's a patio, not a room, and there's a chaise in the center and the guy she's with, one of her husbands, he sort of supports her across the patio and she plops down on this chaise and she says what she wants to drink and he goes off to get it.

"I'm in the corner now, remember, and she's sitting all alone in the center of this patio and for a minute there was nothing. And then this crazy thing started to happen: every fag in the place—every guy you'd heard whispered about, all these stars they left the girls they were with and started a mass move toward Garland. She didn't ask for it. She was just sitting there blinking in the sun while this thing happened, all these beautiful men, some of them big stars, some of them not so big, they circled her, crowded around her, and pretty soon she'd disappeared, gone behind this expensive male fence.

"It may not sound like all that much, but I'm telling you she magnetized them. I'll never forget all those famous secret guys moving across this gorgeous patio without a sound. And her sitting there, kind of blinking, and then they were on her and she was gone. . . ."

Shana Alexander

FROM *LIFE* MAGAZINE   JUNE 2, 1961

Judy's New Rainbow

Old troubles behind her, a great star is now reborn.

Up a dark alley to the stage door hurries a strange little creature bundled in mink from ears to ankles. In the dim light it looks like a fur shmoo wearing a topknot of hair curlers.

Inside the jam-packed theater tension hangs like a net between the audience and the big orchestra on stage. The overture begins, and one by one all the familiar hoped-for melodies come flooding back. Each time the musicians launch a new one across the footlights fans send back salvos of applause, and with every volley the emotional pressure inside the hall rises a few more degrees. Finally the vast space above the audience shimmers with visions of clanging trolley cars, men that got away and birds flying over the rainbow. At this point in the series of identical musical evenings which have taken place recently in 14 major U.S. cities, a plump little 38-year-old woman hiding behind furls of dusty curtain knows it is again time to go to work, and to deafening billows of applause, which drown out the orchestra's final crashing chords, Miss Judy Garland trots cheerfully to center stage.

The uproar subsides, the songs begin. ". . . So keep on smiling, 'cause when you're SMILING . . ." At first the audience cannot believe it will last. "You *go* to my head. . . . I could cry—salty tears—" The big, sobby voice flows out unrestrained across the footlights, rich as caramel, solid as lava. This is the *old* Judy Garland voice. ". . . Who cares what banks *fail* in Yonkers, long as you've got a kiss that CONquers?" She's strutting now, balancing on the slender legs and prancing like a pony. At the end of Act One comes a performance of *San Francisco* so brassy, so sassy, delivered with such a full head of steam that one expects the whole theater to pull away from the levee and start churning down river under its own power.

More than a concert is under way in this hall now; it is a tribal celebration. "I—can't—give—you—anything but love, baby. . . ." After the first four notes everybody recognizes the song at the same instant, and 4,000 people gasp with pleasure. The hot, solid voice speaks personally to each listener until the entire audience has been hypnotized into one huge multi-celled organism. The tribal celebration takes on overtones of a mystical experience. "I'm gonna love you like nobody's loved you . . . I'm gonna *love* you, I'm gonna *love* you . . ." Then the Vesuvius of torch songs, *Stormy Weather,* sung with tears in her voice, her eyes, her throat, running down her neck. By the end of Act Two ("*Zing* went the *strings.* . . . Clang, clang, clang! . . . Rock-a-bye your bay-BEE! . . .") she has the crowd on its feet, shouting and swaying down the aisles, reaching up over the footlights to touch her hand. Comes the final heart-stopping cry of innocence and unbearable longing, "Why then, oh why . . . can't . . . I?" and on some nights the true believers come swarming up onto the stage like lemmings.

It is over. The tribe staggers homeward to sleep off the magic spell. When they awaken they are a tribe no longer, just individuals, tinker, tailor, soldier, sailor, and nobody can quite say what the uproar was all about. Yet the next time Judy Garland walks out on stage in another town to face thousands of different people, the same thing will happen again. And if she doesn't appear for five years or 10, they will still remember and still pack the theater in hopes that the magic will come again. And if she can't sing another note, they will stand in the aisles and shout, "We love you, Judy!" and "Just stand there, Judy!" For Judy Garland today is not only the most electrifying entertainer to watch on stage since Al Jolson. She has moved beyond talent and beyond fame to become the rarest phenomenon in all show business: part bluebird, part phoenix, she is a legend in her own time.

Sometimes in the evangelical frenzy of her finale, as the crowds scream hoarsely for "More! More! We love you! We want more!" one gets the feeling that Judy Garland may be about to cut a vein. By temperament she is incapable of holding anything of herself in reserve. This gives her performance an old-fashioned theatrical excitement, as if a shower of Roman candles were coming over the footlights. It is a style marvelously florid in this cool electronic era of entertainment. For Garland fans her great warmth and responsiveness generate the enormous emotional identification that each listener feels for Judy personally. It is what Spencer Tracy is talking about when he says, "A Garland audience doesn't just listen, they feel. They have their arms around her when she works." It is an all-out, go-for-broke performance that takes everything to give.

Seen from backstage, Judy sometimes suggests a calliope that has been mortally wounded. At intermission she staggers to her dressing room, gasping and clutching her middle, panting that she cannot possibly finish the show, she is too exhausted, too hot, there is a dagger in her throat. She tears off her soggy costume and sips a glass of white wine as her hairdresser blows icy air over her heaving back and shoulders with a portable dryer. But 10 minutes later, the streaked make-up restored, the limp hairdo repuffed, she is zipped into the next costume and ready to go back to work. Often visitors comment on Judy's powers of physical recovery. "Well, you know, I'm like Rocky Graziano," she says amiably, and with a little giggle she scampers back toward the stage.

When she comes off at the end of her show, she sometimes must be helped to her dressing room. Sprawled on a couch in her fuzzy blue robe (a sentimental talisman from her daughter, Liza), waiting for enough strength to flow back so that she can dress and make her way through the huge crowd gathering now at the stage door, Judy talks about what it feels like to face the kind of frenzied, revivalist receptions she has been getting.

"You stand there in the wings," she reflects, "and sometimes you want to yell because the band sounds so good. Then you walk out and if it's a really great audience, a very strange set of emotions can come over you. You don't know what to do. It's a combination of feeling like Queen Victoria and an absolute ass. Sometimes a great reception—though God knows I've had some great receptions and I ought to be prepared for it by now—can really throw you. It kind of shatters you so that you can lose control of your voice and it takes two or three numbers to get back into your stride. I lift my hand in a big gesture in the middle of my first number and if I *see* it's not trembling then I know I haven't lost control.

"A really great reception makes me feel like I have a great big warm heating pad all over me. People en masse have always been wonderful to me. I truly have a great love for an audience, and I used to want to prove it to them by giving them blood. But I have a funny new thing now, a real determination to *make* people enjoy the show. I want to give them two hours of just *pow!*"

This all-out quality, this determination to give everything she has, is a trait that Judy was born with. It is the secret of her success as a performer and it lies at the heart of the Garland legend. But it has taken a lifetime in show business for Judy to learn how to give a maximum of *pow!* with a minimum of blood, and in the course of her 35-year-long lesson in this difficult art, the woman behind the legend has many times come close to destruction.

Judy, whose real name is Frances Ethel Gumm, has been a professional singer since the night she dashed on stage at the Grand Theater in Grand Rapids, Minn., where her family's small-time vaudeville act was booked for Christmas week, and sang two impromptu choruses of *Jingle Bells*. She was 2½ years old, and thereafter she toured as the youngest of the Gumm Sisters. "I had great fun as a little girl," Judy says today. "We played games backstage. Then I went on, sang, took bows, came off and had my mother do my ringlets up again. People always applauded and it was all rather pleasant."

It was very much less pleasant when, at 12, she became a child movie star at M-G-M. For 11 years, after her triumph in *The Wizard of Oz*, though audiences clung to her image as an innocent child skipping along the yellow brick road without a care in the world, she was in reality keeping pace with the most backbreaking production schedule in Hollywood history. While she was still in her teens she completed 12 pictures, nearly all of them long, difficult, exhausting song-and-dance extravaganzas. On film the result was wonderful: from *Strike Up the Band* through *For Me and My Gal, Meet Me in St. Louis* and *Easter Parade*, she was about the nicest, prettiest, most talented minstrel girl a moviegoer could hope to see.

But the making of the movie star very nearly crippled the girl. M-G-M was cashing in as often and as fast as it could, and nobody worked harder at becoming a star than Judy herself. By driving herself mercilessly, by loading up with stimulants to keep going and then with sleeping pills to relax, she managed to make 30 movies for her studio, every one of them with a high professional sheen. But between pictures, instead of the vacations she needed, she began having nervous breakdowns. Before she was 23 years old she had had three breakdowns and two marriages, first to bandleader David Rose, then to director Vincente Minnelli.

Under the relentless necessity of laying golden eggs for M-G-M she became a frazzled song-and-dance zombie. She was difficult, impossible. There was a series of suspensions, recriminations, tears, forgiveness, brief rest periods, then more work, more breakdowns.

On June 17, 1950, after she failed to report for a Saturday dance rehearsal with Fred Astaire, the studio suspended her for the third time. Despondent and frantic, M-G-M's prize goose dashed into the bathroom and slashed her neck with a broken water glass, and the golden eggs stopped.

A few months later "for her own best interests" the studio released her from her contract. She was considered unemployable. Her salary had not been high by Hollywood standards, and her frequent breakdowns plus the normal movie star's expenses had taken all she earned. Her second marriage had just fallen apart. She was 28 years old.

"After I was thrown out of Metro, I really went to pieces for a while," Judy says today. "All I wanted to do was eat and hide. I lost all my self-confidence. For 10 years I was afraid of stores, planes, cars. When I worked, I suffered agonies of stage fright. People had literally to push me out on stage." The person who did the pushing and at times was able to restore Judy's sagging confidence in herself both as a woman and as a performer was Sid Luft, a onetime test pilot for Douglas Aircraft. Luft became Judy's manager, then her husband.

Under Luft's stewardship Judy began making more comebacks than a yo-yo. Over a period of nearly 10 years she played the Palladium, the Palace, nightclubs, theaters. Everywhere she went she drew record crowds and large grosses. She and Luft made their own movie, *A Star Is Born,* and some critics called it the finest musical ever to come out of Hollywood. She did a TV show for the biggest audience in history. She had already had one daughter, Liza Minnelli, and she and Luft had two more children, Lorna and Joseph.

But between the high points came many lows. She was obviously often ill; she couldn't pay her bills; there were rumors that she was a hopeless alcoholic, a drug addict; she didn't show up for work, she collapsed on stage, she lost her voice, she lost her figure, she fought with everybody. But it was during these same years of violent ups and downs that the public image of Garland as the bluebird really began to take wing. The struggles of the woman, no longer hidden by the smokescreen of studio publicity, were the making of the legend.

By 1958 and 1959 the Garland yo-yo had begun to lose its resiliency. The great voice had perceptibly begun to fail along with everything else, and though people by the thousands still came to see her, all they saw on stage some nights was a dumpy woman singing a quavery lullaby. Neither Judy nor her public knew how sick she really was. "Sometimes I felt as if I was performing in a blizzard," she says today. At other times she would suddenly feel nauseated or dizzy in the middle of her performance. This was a new terror. "You are never so *alone* as when you are ill on stage. The most nightmarish feeling in the world is suddenly to feel like throwing up in front of 4,000 people."

By autumn of 1959 Judy was unable to work at all. She felt frightened, sick and mentally confused. In late November she was admitted to a hospital in New York City. She looked awful. Her face was a puffy white mask. Her eyes were glazed, she felt faint, she couldn't remember things. Her whole body was grossly fat and bloated. Her limbs were so stiff and swollen that sometimes she could barely move, and at other times she trembled uncontrollably. She was clapped into bed at once, and batteries of tests were begun.

All her alarming symptoms, including the mental ones, turned out to have a real physical basis. The doctors said she had hepatitis and that it was due, at least in part, to the combined effects of certain tranquilizers and diet pills which previous doctors, treating previous breakdowns, had prescribed for her. The new doctors guessed she might have been walking around with hepatitis for as long as three years. The patient admitted she had swallowed a great many drugs over the past 15 years, careening and ricocheting between sleeping pills and pep pills, diet medicines and nerve tonics, in her struggle for physical and emotional stability.

There were many puzzling symptoms to her latest collapse, and as the weeks dragged on, platoons of specialists were summoned to review her case. Finally one day the chief specialist appeared at her bedside. Behind him stood Sid Luft, looking equally grave. "Miss Garland, you are still a young woman and I wish I did not have to tell you this," the doctor said. "But I have no choice. For the rest of your life all your physical activity must be curtailed. Everything you eat and drink must be strictly regulated. You must learn to accept the fact that you are a *permanent* semi-invalid. It goes without saying that under no circumstances can you ever work again."

Up to that moment it had been a classic Hollywood bedside scene. Then the patient spoke. "Whoopee!" she cried weakly and fell back among the pillows.

After five months of hospital care she then spent four more months convalescing at her home in Beverly Hills. She appeared publicly for the first time in July to campaign for her friend, Jack Kennedy, and then rather suddenly she flew off to England alone.

The flight was the first sign that Judy Garland might have recovered from something more than hepatitis. Her fear of airplanes had once been so severe that she could not go near an airport without trembling. As Judy herself tells the story today, "When the doctor told me that work was out of the question for me forever, I felt greatly relieved. The pressure was off me for the first time in my life. Physically I recovered rather well because I am a terribly strong woman, but I knew I had to get out of California. I was liked in California but nobody needed me. The phone never rang. In Hollywood I was somebody who *had been* a movie star."

In England she told the British press she hoped to settle there permanently. Her husband was detained in the United States but would join her in a few weeks. So would her three children. She took a town house, bought a dog, took steps to enroll the children in English schools and put her Beverly Hills house up for sale. She shopped in Mayfair and fed the pigeons in Trafalgar Square. Life as a nonworking semi-invalid was turning out to be every bit as pleasant as she had hoped. She still looked chubby but the unhealthy bloat had almost disappeared. By early autumn of 1960 she was feeling better than she had in years.

One sleepless night in London (she still suffered, as she had all her life, from galloping insomnia) she got out of bed, locked herself in the bathroom, turned on the hot shower full blast—both to drown out the sound of her voice and to pamper her long-unused throat with live steam—and began to run through some of her old arrangements. Twenty minutes later she flung open the door, shook her groggy husband awake and, still steaming faintly, read him a list of some 30-odd songs. "Are you sure it isn't too much?" he inquired, recalling the doctor's warning.

"Too much?" repeated Judy in a newly steamed voice that could carry to the second balcony. "If I die we'll know it's too much! That specialist! Where'd they import *him* from, Transylvania?" It must have been clear to sleepers for blocks around that Judy Garland was ready to go back to work.

Judy played her new show at the Palladium on Aug. 28, 1960, and, in her words, "It was a pistol!" She played the show in the provinces thereafter and a few times on the Continent. "My work was not going in any particular direction," she says now, "but I didn't care. I seemed to have a brandnew life." In her new life Judy Garland the performer was for the first time playing second fiddle to a high-spirited housewife with the horrible name of Frances Ethel Gumm Luft. As F. E. G. Luft, "I was terribly happy personally. I immensely enjoyed taking my kids to Battersea Park. I looked forward to the days. It sounds so corny to say it, but I felt reborn."

At the same time that Judy was being reborn in England, a Music Corporation of America talent agent in New York named Freddie Fields decided it was time to get reborn himself. Fields cut loose from M.C.A. and went into business on his own as a combination personal manager, business manager and agent for "a few select clients." Judy Garland, he knew from the show business grapevine, was in England, semiretired, personally happy but professionally drifting. What a challenge for a fledgling impresario! He obtained an appointment with Judy and flew to London.

The meeting was a pistol too. "With Freddie, something clicked," Judy says. "He seemed to know how to do exactly what I could not do: channel my work." Returning to New York, Fields cut back the underbrush of a lifetime of managerial untidiness:

- He settled his new client's three-year legal battle with CBS and negotiated a giant new TV spectacular.

- He got her a starring role in a big new Hollywood movie, *Judgment at Nuremberg.*

- He booked her for a 14-city, six-week U.S. concert tour, which was the quickest way simultaneously to prove to both the singer and her public that no one in the business could create as much pure theatrical excitement as Judy Garland, and also to begin paying off a huge pile of old bills.

Four months ago in Dallas the phoenix aspect of the Garland legend was revealed to a U.S. audience for the first time. She gave the same show she had programmed in the shower. It lasted 2¼ hours, left her shaking with fatigue, earned her two standing ovations and a newspaper review that began, with Texas grandeur and simplicity, "No entertainer has ever given such a show in Dallas. . . ." Two nights later in Houston she gave the same show, got four standing ovations and, except for the geographical change, the same review: ". . . unquestionably the greatest show ever given in Houston."

Buoyed by Texas, Judy Garland went before a Hollywood camera this spring for the first time in six years to play the most un-Garland role ever invented—a drab little German *Hausfrau* and onetime victim of Nazi persecution who returns to Nuremberg to testify against her old tormentors. Any actress would think twice before accepting the *Hausfrau* role: it was totally unglamorous, technically demanding and she would be playing against such giants as Spencer Tracy, Burt Lancaster, Richard Widmark and Maximilian Schell, all of whom have important assignments in the same scene. For Judy in particular, the part seemed an insanity: she would not sing a note, she would be on screen for only nine minutes, and the salary was $50,000, a tiny fraction of what she used to be paid. Yet despite all obstacles, Judy and Fields realized that Hollywood needed fast, dramatic proof that Garland was a dependable, professional actress after all.

On her first day on the *Nuremberg* set, in the first scene of the day, *Hausfrau* Garland was required to burst into tears. As the cameras ground away, the actors did the scene once, twice, a third time. Finally in the middle of the sixth take Judy suddenly scowled, stamped her foot angrily and walked off the set. The entire crew froze: so it was just like the old days at M-G-M.

But it was not like the old days at all. As Judy explained it to Director Kramer, "Damn it, Stanley, I can't do it. I've dried up. I'm too happy today to cry." Kramer called a 10-minute break, Garland retired to her dressing room to discompose herself, and when shooting resumed she was able to weep.

The night before she left Hollywood Judy went to a small party given by old friends. During the evening Kramer telephoned from his office at the studio. He, Tracy, Widmark and Screenwriter Abby Mann had just reviewed the completed footage of her scenes for the first time. When the sequence ended, Kramer told her, the four men had stood up all alone in the little projection room and burst into applause. At this news Judy shed her first real tears since coming back to her home town. She was completely ready in every way for the brutal but profitable concert tour.

Judy's financial objective these days is to pay off her old debts, then establish some trust funds for her three children. Alan Jay Lerner and Richard Rodgers hope to write a Broadway musical version of *Roman Holiday* for her. She is working on an autobiography of her first 38 years and Capitol Records will soon bring out *Judy at Carnegie Hall*. She will tape a TV spectacular and has scheduled more concert dates. But that's not all: among those negotiating for her services is, of all companies, M-G-M. Her total earnings for this year should be approximately a million dollars. After taxes, expenses and old bills are paid, she will begin to see some of what managers call "keeping money" for the first time in years.

From then on the chief beneficiaries of the Garland legend will be the three people in the world who are least interested in that legend and most interested in the woman herself: namely, Liza, Lorna and Joe. This state of affairs is just fine with Judy, a devoted and skillful parent who, despite her own troubled past, has managed to raise a trio of remarkably untroubled and charming children. Sometimes when work forces her to be away from them, Judy says, "I have *no* ambition to be an actress, *no* ambition to be a singer, I have absolutely no drive. I just want to be a mother." But Judy does not envisage complete retirement, even when her debts are paid and her children provided for. She simply would prefer to work less often and under circumstances that she could control. So far, such control is a luxury she cannot afford.

The most grueling form of show business ever invented is the one-night stand, whether the performer is a third-rate juggler or a big star like Judy Garland. As the tour progresses, the physical wear and tear tends to increase. In addition to the intense physical exertion on stage (Judy works so hard that her heavy clothes drop to the dressing room floor at the end of each act like suits of soggy armor), there are all the normal off-stage touring problems of getting star, manager David Begelman, conductor, three musicians, a hairdresser and a secretary all transported from city to city every second day, on and off trains, in and out of hotels, taxied back and forth to theaters, seeing that everybody is fed, housed, rehearsed and paid, and keeping track of a mountain of luggage packed with everything from tom-toms to chicken soup. The logistics of all this are carefully planned well in advance of the tour, and none of it is supposed to worry

Judy. Her job is to sing, which is like saying that Sir Edmund Hillary's job was to climb.

Actually she becomes involved in everything. One night when the entourage arrived at the railroad station, a strip of red carpet was stretched across the tobacco-stained marble floor. The proud stationmaster was on hand to greet Miss Garland and invite her to wait in his private office until train time when he would personally escort her to her compartment. Judy said she would be delighted. A short while later the dispatcher wandered by and complained that he was having an awful time announcing trains lately. His throat hurt all the time.

"You're probably not using your voice right," Judy said. "Take a deep breath and I'll show you." The mink-coated star took hold of the startled dispatcher and pushed hard against his belly. "Feel it? *That's* where your power comes from." She gave him a light punch in the diaphragm. "And be very careful of those loud *eee* sounds. They'll give you a bleeding throat unless you keep your teeth open."

Judy copes with her own professional problems with equal efficiency and not much can happen in front of an audience that will faze her. Musically she depends on her conductor, Mort Lindsey, and three permanent musicians (a jazz drummer, a bongo player and a first trumpet) to weld the 25-man local orchestras into a unit during the meticulous six-hour rehearsals that precede every concert. The orchestral surprises that do occur are usually caused by Judy's own sudden powerful impact on the local musicians.

In one city, right in the midst of her blood-vessel-bursting final chorus of *Swanee,* the brass section was so astonished by Judy's lung power that several men stopped playing and listened. In Buffalo a musician rose in the middle of a number, opened his coat, focused a camera dangling against his chest, clicked, wound, buttoned up, sat down and got his viola back under his chin in time for his next passage.

If there are surprises during a performance, Judy lives through them. One night during *Over the Rainbow,* standing on a blocked-out stage in front of 8,000 people, many of them sniffing audibly, her face illuminated by a single dramatic pin-spot, her eyes brimming with tears, she got as far as ". . . way up high—There's a land that I heard of . . ." when a rather large moth flew into her open mouth. With a flick of her tongue she tucked the moth into her cheek, sang her way perfectly through the next 28 bars while waiting for the blackout, then coughed, spit and stomped.

When the lights came up she was seen bowing and smiling like a seraph through her tears.

Naturally enough Judy has occasional sore throats, and she knows from experience that the only balm and restorative is live steam. This commodity being sometimes hard to come by in a hotel room, she travels with a hot plate and a steam kettle for emergency treatments. But if a hotel does have good hot water in its pipes, she likes to take advantage of it. Before a performance she often spends an hour or more in a steam-filled bathroom, reclining on a pile of sofa pillows like some small Turkish odalisque, writing postcards to her children and tidily steaming out her collection of knitted travel outfits which hang from the shower rod like a frieze of misty banners.

Her hotel room is also the setting for her continuing and incredibly complex battles with insomnia. The strain of giving people two hours of "just *pow!*" every other night makes it very difficult for Judy to unwind afterward, and her main problem on tour is to get enough rest or, on many nights, to get any sleep at all. Dinner may last until 1 A.M. and there is always the *Late Late Show* but then, as any insomniac knows, come the desperate hours.

On tour Judy is no ordinary insomniac. She cannot take sleeping medicines because, when she awakens, she would be too "down" to perform, and if she then took a pep pill to get "up," her vibrato would go. Sometimes during the desperate hours, despite the steamings, despite all care, she can feel her throat closing up *right now!* What to do? Strong magic is needed. At these times Judy, the woman, must force herself to become the abject handmaiden of Judy, the insomniac singer. Ah-ha, she will take the singer for a nice invigorating walk in the beautiful dawn! She dresses and goes outside. She returns invigorated, almost sleepy, but now hungry too. Suddenly she's positive she could fall asleep if only she had a nice hot bowl of Chinese egg-flower soup. She has arrived at the true black magic stage; she knows it, she has been here before and she is rather niftily prepared.

"The main problem when practicing witchcraft in strange hotel rooms," as Judy said later when telling this story, "is not to let room service notice anything unusual." At 6:30 one morning she plugged in her bathroom hot plate, rummaged in her luggage until she found a can of chicken noodle soup, found a beer can opener and went to work. After half an hour's intense concentration she got most of the noodles through the hole in the can lid. She sprinkled in some seasoning, also from her luggage, and set the soup to simmer. Now she needed only a raw egg and a soup bowl. This was easy. She telephoned room service and gave a very precise breakfast order: "This is Miss Garland speaking. I would like a glass of orange juice and some dry cereal please. Any kind. No, nothing else. . . . Oh, I almost forgot. I like a raw egg in my orange juice, but I will put in the egg *myself*." When the order arrived, Judy discarded the orange juice (which gives her hives) and the cereal (which she has not tasted in 20 years), assembled her soup, drank it and drifted off at last to sleep.

The amount of sleep she is able to get varies but the ritual of getting ready for the next show does not. By the time she has to leave for the theater, Judy has already been fed (lamb chops and tea), coiffeured (by her traveling hairdresser), meticulously made up (by herself—short, medium or long eyelashes, depending on the size of the theater), and soothed by a manager who says the acoustics are superb and by a conductor who swears that *this* band really swings. Her secretary has packed the giant suitcase with two complete changes of clothes, several spare pairs of sheer black nylons in the smallest size made and a stack of towels for mopping up. Another bag holds a sack of ice cubes, some tumblers and a bottle or two of chilled white wine. The alcohol Judy is now permitted to drink is diluted *Liebfraumilch*, and she likes to keep a supply in her dressing room. While she is on stage, a friend stands by in the wings with an emergency glassful in case her throat should suddenly go dry between numbers.

By 8:50 P.M. at the theater the overture is pounding forward and the star is dressed and waiting edgily in the darkened wings, borrowing a drag on somebody's cigarette, nibbling a mint, taking a last sip of *Liebfraumilch*-on-the-rocks and chattering inanely: "Well, what'll we all *do* for the next two hours?" The orchestra cannonballs toward its climax and just a few feet away the bass drum pounds its portentous rhythm: ". . . the road gets *rougher*, it's lonelier and *tougher*. . . ." Without warning, Judy Garland suddenly turns her back on the watchers in the wings, sets her shoulders, takes what seems like a 10-gallon deep breath and then—astonishingly, as one looks out from the darkness directly into the footlights' glare—she appears to glide away onto the bright-lit stage like a child's pull toy, powered by the rising wave of the applause itself.

The Comeback Kid

The pre-eminent date of the tour was Carnegie Hall on April 23 [1961]. And all available tickets had been bought within hours of going on sale. There was a "buzz" in New York about the "new" Judy Garland. Outside the theatre, touts were demanding $500 a ticket as the doors remained closed until minutes before the curtain was due to rise. This led to the dreadful speculation that the star was not going to appear. She had, in fact, been in her dressing room since five, petrified by fear and damned if she was going to go on.

Among those in the audience were Spencer Tracy, Julie Andrews, Lauren Bacall and Jason Robards (whom she married a few weeks later), Henry Fonda, Rock Hudson, Leonard Bernstein, Anthony Perkins, Eli Wallach and Anne Jackson, Hedda Hopper, Richard Burton, Carol Channing, Myrna Loy, Mike Nichols, Dore Schary, Merv Griffin, and Henny Youngman—who was standing because he could not get a seat.

—David Shipman in *Judy Garland: The Secret Life of an American Legend*

Bill Davidson

FROM *McCALL'S*   JANUARY 1962

Judy: Another Look at the Rainbow

I sat in the Hollywood Bowl with Jerry Lewis and his wife, Patti, and it was raining, and we were soaked to the skin. But along with eighteen thousand other people, who filled the huge amphitheater from rim to rim, we did not move to take shelter from the steady drizzle, because we could not take our eyes from the lone figure on the stage, who commanded every facet of our attention. The rain fell on her, too, and it matted the fabric of the unbecoming sequined blouse she was wearing, and her make-up smeared on the puffy flesh of her cheeks, and the matronly fat showed through the ill-fitting black slacks. But it was Judy Garland singing there, and she did something to all of us, and when it was over we were standing on our seats, shouting, "Bravo!" Almost ashamed of my reaction I asked Lewis, "Did you ever do that before for any performer?" And he said, "No, but I don't think any of these people ever did *that* before, either." He pointed to the stage, where hundreds of jaded denizens of the film colony were pressing forward just to touch Miss Garland's hand.

What happened in Hollywood last September also happened in New York City's Carnegie Hall, in London's Palladium, Paris' Palais de Chaillot, in Dallas, Houston, and eleven other American cities. Last spring, when Miss Garland reported for work in her first movie in six years, Stanley Kramer's picture *Judgment at Nuremberg*, the crew—many of whom she had antagonized with her irresponsibility and her demeaning attitude in

past productions—gave her a standing ovation as she appeared on Universal's Sound Stage Nine. When the picture was sneak-previewed at the United Artists Theater in San Francisco and at the Palace Theater in New York, the audiences greeted the names of her costars—Burt Lancaster, Spencer Tracy, Richard Widmark, Maximilian Schell, Montgomery Clift and Marlene Dietrich—with silence. When *her* name appeared in the credits, both theaters rocked with unexpected applause, before even a foot of film had been shown. Prior to the opening of the film at the Pantages Theater, in Hollywood, three six-foot photographs of her were stolen from the theater's lobby.

The Judy Garland comeback story is one of the most astounding phenomena in show business today. No one can satisfactorily explain it. Eighteen months ago, her long, troubled career seemed to be over. She had lost her two-decade battle against overweight, and the appealing little wide-eyed girl of *The Wizard of Oz* no longer was discernible in the excess of flesh that encased her. The face was lined with years of unrestrained living, multiple neuroses, insomnia, and pill taking. The endearing voice had cracked. Her third marriage seemed to be on the rocks. Inundated by a small army of creditors in the United States, she had fled to England with her three children and was living there as Frances Gumm Luft, housewife.

It is not our purpose to dig into Miss Garland's past to unearth the sordidness, regimentation, breakdowns, and frustration that led to her premature obsolescence in 1959, when she was only thirty-seven years old. That story can be told only by Miss Garland herself. What we are concerned with here is the incredible Judy Garland of 1962—still overweight, still seeking for peace and stability within herself, but now possessed of a magic quotient that can whip adult audiences into a frenzy of ecstasy as no one in show business or the opera or on the concert stage can do today, not even the teenage idols like Paul Anka and Bobby Darin, with their manipulated mob-claques of lovelorn adolescents. With Judy, there are no contrivances, no paid swooners, no press agentry. She can't even afford a regular publicist or advertising ballyhoo. When the people turn out to see her perform, they come with nothing but affection and respect—and, perhaps, memory.

What *is* the new magic quotient that has such a hypnotic effect on her audiences? I first became exposed to it when I went to the Copacabana in New York last winter to see a closing-night performance by Sammy Davis, Jr. The nightclub was filled with celebrities—a sort of show-business tribal custom for closing nights—and when Davis' show was over, I settled back for the usual long set of introductions and bows by Louella Parsons, Victor Jory, Brenda Lee, William Bendix, and the like. But as Davis stood before the microphone, there was a strange look on his face, and I sensed that something unusual was coming. He said, "Ladies and gentlemen, tonight I want to dispense with show business tradition and just introduce two great ladies in the audience. The first is my mother." (Mrs. Davis stood up to be greeted by polite applause.) Then Davis continued: "The second great lady has just returned to New York from London, where she has been recovering from a serious illness. Her name is—Judy Garland."

For an instant, the audience in the jam-packed room was silent. Then came the applause, accompanied by a noise that seemed to be a wail as hundreds of throats emitted "Oh" simultaneously. A baby spotlight picked out the dumpy little figure, in a white blouse and black skirt sitting at a side table, and everyone in the place was on his feet, shouting, "Judy! Judy!" She walked to the microphone, and she wept, and the audience wept, and the musicians wept—and one of them began playing the first bars of "Over the Rainbow," and the others picked it up, and suddenly, almost against her will, Judy Garland was singing before an audience in the United States for the first time in nearly a year. When she reached the high notes at the end—where she sings, "Why, oh, why can't I?"—the audience was so hushed that I could hear a woman behind me praying softly, "Please, *please,* let her make it." She made it, and the audience, on its feet again, called her back for an encore (which she didn't attempt) and seven bows (which she did).

With her ego and confidence buttressed by those magic moments at the Copa, Miss Garland went on to her triumphs of induced audience hysteria at the Hollywood Bowl, Carnegie Hall, etc. Ever since, show-business philosophers have been attempting to diagnose the phenomenon of her almost mystic revival. Sammy Davis, Jr. says, "It's the same thing that happened when Frank Sinatra came back after he seemed to be down for the count. People like to see the champ get up off the floor to score a knockout." Jerry Lewis probes a little deeper. He told me: "People now know the trouble Judy has been through. Who among us isn't plagued with trouble, too? So people of all kinds, with worries and problems and heartaches, go to see her, and they identify with her. And when she sings, she is communicating for them all the emotions they can't communicate themselves because they don't have a stage and a microphone and talent. The stout women in the audience identify with her, and the insomniacs in the audience identify with her, and the losers-in-love identify with her, and the people who remember their own unhappy childhoods identify with her, and the alcoholics and pill takers identify with her. All the people whose insides have been torn out by misery identify with her—and she is singing for all of them. In a way, she's singing with a hundred voices."

Movie producer Stanley Kramer disagrees. "Sure she's got the sympathy and the audience identifies with her," he says, "but two other major factors seem even more important to me. First of all, she's a great technician. There's nobody in the entertainment world today, actor or singer, who can run the complete range of emotions, from utter pathos to power and dimension, the way she can. In this respect, she's the greatest all-around entertainer since Al Jolson, who could break into one of the old standards, as phony as they were in those days, and something happened to the audience, and they participated with him. Judy's the same way. She's like a piano. You touch any key and the pure note of that emotion comes out. She knows how to laugh and cry on cue. When we made *Judgment at Nuremberg,* I'd just have to say, 'Judy, register hate and fear, like a German *Hausfrau* who had been persecuted by the Nazis,' and the hate and fear would be there. It's the same thing when she's doing a concert, and she ends the show by sitting on the edge of the stage and singing 'Over the Rainbow.' She hits the lachrymal key on her piano, and the tears come out—and she cries, and the audience cries.

"But," continues Kramer, "there's another attribute she seems to have acquired lately. Maybe it was the last siege of misfortune that did it: but when she stands up there before an audience now, she has the dignity of a woman who has been through it all and knows what it's all about. The people sense this new dignity and respond to it. More than anything else, I think, this accounts for that incredible mass neurosis of reaction she seems to start whenever she's onstage."

This feeling of dignity was a long time in coming. As everyone knows, Judy was thrust on the stage by her parents when she was two years old. When other kids were growing up normally in kindergarten and elementary school, she was touring the country as part of a vaudeville team known as the Gumm Sisters (she was born Frances Ethel Gumm). She had a relentless stage mother, a weak father, who died when she was quite young, and then came the cruel paternalism of the movies, which drained her energy by robbing her of her adolescence and converting her into what she calls "a moneymaking machine who was not expected to have human emotions."

There were two bad marriages (partially manipulated by the studio) to orchestra leader David Rose and to movie director Vincente Minnelli, and then the machine began to break down. Judy rebelled against the constant dieting to lick the overweight problem that had plagued her since she was a teenager. She began to show up late to work for her pictures. She became surly and temperamental on the set, and finally she walked out on pictures completely. In 1950, after she failed to appear for a dance rehearsal with Fred Astaire for *The Barclays of Broadway,* she was suspended and slashed her neck with a broken water glass. A few months later, she walked out of *Annie Get Your Gun,* and the studio sent her for a rest cure in a Boston hospital. But when she failed to report for *Royal Wedding,* she was finished. Her contract with the studio was canceled once and for all.

After that came several years of ups and downs—and recurrent misery. She married Sid Luft, an ex-test pilot turned agent, who became her business manager. Luft helped her get started doing her personal appearance concerts and put her into the movie *A Star Is Born,* in which she scored a critical but not a financial success. By now, her friends were all the misfits of Hollywood, and they tried to cheer her on with their roistering parties whenever she opened in one of her variety shows. But the roistering did her no good. Neither did the constant diet of pills and medications she consumed to slim her down, to give her energy, to help her sleep, and to wake her up. She developed fears about flying in airplanes, fears about appearing in public with her bloated figure, fears about eating certain foods that gave her allergies, fears about not being able to fall asleep, fears about not being able to stay awake, fears about going into stores to do simple shopping. After all her years in show business, she fell prey to such an acute stage fright that Luft often literally had to push her on to the stage to perform. At every show, she perspired so profusely that she required several changes of costume. "And then," she says, "came the worst thing of all. I began to feel nauseated in the middle of a performance."

In the fall of 1959, the voice suddenly was gone. The lovely high notes had become a quaver, and she knew she had had it. She checked into a New York hospital, and after an exhaustive series of tests, it was discovered that she was suffering from hepatitis. She was put on a strict diet, was forbidden ever to drink alcoholic beverages except for an occasional sip of diluted wine, and was told she would never be able to work again. That's when she fled to England and became Mrs. Luft, housewife and mother.

After six months of rest and total attention to her three children—Liza, Lorna and Joe—the voice suddenly came back. She tried it out in a performance at the Palladium, in London, in August, 1960, and when it worked, she went on a European tour and then, in New York, made that fortuitous appearance at Sammy Davis' closing night at the Copacabana. From that point on, under the guidance of a new manager, Freddie Fields, everything went well for her professionally.

Her problems, however, are not yet over. She still suffers from stage fright, and she emerges drenched from each performance. She still finds it difficult to fall asleep at night, and certain foods still give her hives. The never-ending battle against excess weight has not been won. She still weeps, sometimes in the loneliness of her dressing room.

But a strong metamorphosis in Judy has enabled her to function again as an artist and a woman. It seems to be the result of a fascinating chain reaction that has taken place in her relations with her audience, the people who pay up to twenty dollars a ticket to watch her perform.

The first link in the chain reaction was forged when the public realized that Judy is a woman with multiple, complex problems. This realization was a long time in coming because of the uncanny effectiveness of the movies' propaganda machine, which was geared to mask any unpleasantness and to build up phony images of its stars. Thus, in the press releases, Judy was incessantly portrayed as a happy, carefree child, so that even after she was a woman in her thirties, with a record of two divorces and three breakdowns, fans would say, "What a nice kid that Judy is. But she should go on a diet and lose a few pounds." It wasn't until recently that it began to dawn on the public that Judy was anything but a happy, carefree kid. It took that long to dispel the unreal image created by the publicists, and it was only her 1959 collapse and disappearance from the show-business scene that, at long last, brought about the emergence of the real Garland. With this emergence came a wave of sympathy and understanding, never present before.

The second link was made when Judy returned to this country and faced audiences she immediately sensed had this new comprehension of her. According to her close friends, she no longer felt she had to worry about her appearance. People were accepting her for what she was, and the struggle to preserve the Garland image of twenty years before was no longer necessary. Says Charlton Heston, "With this came something that was almost a miracle. Judy found love from across the footlights. All her life, she has had a tremendous desire to be wanted—the same as all of us do—and here, every time she stepped on a stage, she realized that thousands of people loved her and wanted her. So performing was no longer an ordeal; it became an exchange of affection. And she is returning the love with the greatest shows of her life. It is almost like a rebirth."

The third link was formed when Stanley Kramer witnessed the exchange of affection at firsthand in Dallas, Texas, where, as in the Hollywood Bowl, thousands of people stood on their seats in the rain and shouted, "Bravo!" Kramer told me, "I looked around and I saw staid citizens I'd seen for years acting like bobbysoxers at a Fabian–Elvis Presley revival meeting. Also, I was struck by the tremendous emotional range of Judy's performance that night. So a few days later, I went to see her and offered her a part in my movie. The part was only an eighteen-minute one; but it was the first that anybody had offered her in years, and she nearly wept with joy. When she reported for work, she got the same affection and understanding from the crew that she had been getting from her audiences, and she responded to it magnificently. There was no temperament or tardiness, for which she had been so notorious in the old days. She was a thoroughgoing professional, and even an old curmudgeon like Spencer Tracy found her a delight to work with. I'm sure a complete new movie career has opened up for her."

So that's a new Judy Garland. But the old Judy Garland is still there, and more than anything else, it is this fascinating amalgam and the new awareness of it that have endeared her once again to the public. As critic Kenneth Tynan pointed out, "Miss Garland is a squat woman now, and it takes some effort of puckering and wrinkling for her face to achieve the hopeful, trusting smile that first transfixed us. But she can still do it because she incarnates a dream of adolescence and all the pain and nostalgia that go with it. When the voice pours out, as rich and pleading as ever, we know where, and how moved, we are—in the presence of a star, and embarrassed by tears."

Does all this indicate that she has won her struggle? She comes from a show-business heritage of recurrent problems of frustration, unreality, false situations, desire, and need. The exchange of affection with her audiences may not be enough, because the personal complications remain. Her marriage to Sid Luft has been a rocky one, with continuing separations and rumors of divorce. A friend says, "Judy must be wanted every minute of every hour of every day—not just when she's on the stage. It's her lifeblood."

The rainbow Judy sings about has a wide arc, and the happiness at the end of it may prove, for her, to be unattainable. There are those who believe she'll never reach it, although nearly everyone—through "the embarrassment of tears"—hopes that someday she will.

V Memory

Judy Garland Far from Home

PARIS—Among the Hollywood stars who have moved to Europe is Judy Garland, who has taken up residence in London. Miss Garland's press agent asked us if we would like to interview her by telephone and we said we would like to. It was the first interview ever done across the English Channel with Judy Garland.

It went like this:

"Hello, Judy? How are you?"

"I'm fine."

"What are you wearing?"

"A red dressing gown. I'm going to have a cup of tea."

"What else?"

"Cucumber sandwiches."

"No, I mean what else are you wearing?"

"White slippers."

"Is your hair up or down?"

"Down. How are you, dear?"

"I'm fine. I'm wearing a black tie and a . . ."

"What else?"

"Nothing else. I'm not going to have any tea."

There was a pause. Apparently, she was eating a cucumber sandwich.

We asked her: "What happened? Why did you leave Hollywood?"

"Well, you see I've been there for so many years and I like it very much, but I decided it would be nice to live in England—you know, because I wanted the children to go to school in Europe and I'd like to be around with them.

"Liza, my 14-year-old one, is having trouble, though. The educational system in Southern California is behind the English schooling system—it's even behind the New York schooling system and Liza has to have tutoring before an English school will take her."

"What are you going to do over here?"

"I'm going to do concerts and probably make a film or two."

"That will take a year or so?"

"Over a year. I don't know how long I'll stay. It's funny—the papers in America have been writing a lot of mean things about me moving over. They seem to think that I'm a traitor or something."

"They'll soon be calling you a runaway movie star."

"Yes, and they sound very angry, but they shouldn't be. After all, I'm going back there."

"They say most Hollywood movie stars who take up residence in England are not driven home by bad publicity but because there is no central heating."

"We're staying in Carol Reed's house. He doesn't have central heating, but there are stoves in every room. It's real nice and warm.

"Eddie Fisher and Elizabeth Taylor are still looking for a house over here. As a matter of fact, they looked at this one before we did, but they looked at it on a dreary, rainy morning and none of the heaters were on, so they turned it down. When Eddie came over the other day all the heaters were on, and he was mad as hell he didn't take it when he had a chance."

"Do you miss your Hollywood friends?"

"Yes, I miss them, but I have friends over here."

"You'll miss the elections."

"I have an absentee ballot, so I'm going to vote."

"Kennedy?"

"Natch."

"Would you go out campaigning for him if you were in the United States?"

"Oh yes. But it probably wouldn't have meant anything one way or another."

"Maybe you could make a record over there."

"That's an idea. Something like 'Even in Kensington I think of Kennedy.' "

"Are you renting your house in Hollywood?"

"Yes. But I let my staff go. This European trip gave me a good excuse to fire them. I didn't have the nerve to do it before. I think it was good to get away just to give me a chance to get rid of all of them."

"How's the English staff?"

"Very nice, very English. They belong to Carol Reed. The cook is wonderful."

"How's the butler?"

"There is no butler."

"No butler? No wonder Eddie Fisher didn't want the house."

Judy Garland's Sister:
The Happy One in the Family

DALLAS, TEX.

Unless their lawyers settle it out of court, the Judy Garland child custody case will soon come to trial.

Certainly it will develop into one of the most nasty, messy, recriminatory trials of our day.

Lawsuits involving the custody of children are characteristically notorious for bringing out the worst in plaintiff and defendant. The husband tries to prove his wife an unfit mother, and the wife offers refuting evidence depicting her husband as a louse of the first water whose slightest touch would contaminate their children beyond redemption.

In the forthcoming case of *Luft vs. Luft* we have two Hollywood protagonists, both capable of washing in public the most soiled of their private linen, both capable of the most savage in-fighting, both capable of making charges which in the widely publicized end are very likely to damage both of them.

Judy Garland's estranged husband, Sid Luft, 46, is her former personal manager and a man not unknown at the gaming tables of Las Vegas and the race tracks of the nation. In her petition to restrain Luft from visiting their two children, Lorna, 11, and Joe, 8, Judy has charged: "He takes their allowance from them and does not return it."

183

Luft, in turn, accuses Judy of being "mentally unbalanced and emotionally disturbed," and points out: "On at least 3 occasions during 1963 and no less than 20 occasions in previous years, she [Miss Garland] has taken overdoses of barbiturates.

"On six occasions," he continues, "she has attempted suicide by slashing herself on her wrists, elbows or throat."

The above is a typical sample of what will be dredged up from the sewer of scandal.

At this writing, Judy, down to 90 pounds—at one time she hit 150—is located somewhere in London with Mark Herron, 28, an apprentice actor who wears tight trousers and in all probability will never be offered the role of Tarzan in any film.

Luft's lawyers have made a complete study of Herron's background, his friendship with Judy, exactly who is paying for what, and the resultant information could very well make headlines.

Because she doesn't want to see Judy's children used as pawns to satisfy the personal bitterness of two scrapping adults, Virginia Garland Thompson, 47—Judy's only surviving sister—prays devoutly each day that the case of *Luft vs. Luft* will be settled peaceably behind closed doors.

"Judy has had more than her share of troubles in this life," her sister asserts, "and while we've broken away from each other, I still wish her something I've known for years and she hasn't since childhood—peace of mind."

Virginia Thompson, happily married to John Thompson, a special delivery clerk in the U.S. Post Office, lives in Pleasant Grove, Tex., a restful little suburb of Dallas. On a budget of $500 a month she and her husband live in a modern two-bedroom house (with swimming pool) on one green acre of land, far removed from the Hollywood jungle in which Judy Garland lost her way and seemingly a million miles from Las Vegas, where a third Garland sister, Sue, recently took her life via the sleeping pill route.

A few weeks ago, sitting beside her on a sofa in her living room, I asked Virginia Thompson: "How come out of the three Garland sisters, you're the only one who's found happiness? Is it because you got out of Hollywood and show business?"

This attractive, blond Texas housewife ruminated for several moments. "I don't really know," she answered. "I think a woman's happiness depends largely on her choice of a husband. Judy and Sue were always poor judges of men. I was, too, at the beginning, but luckily I improved.

"I don't know that people in show business are more or less happy than those who are not. I do know that show business throws you into contact with exciting, frequently talented and handsome men who don't make particularly good husbands. Actors, musicians, producers, directors—they are almost too creative to be stable."

She then went on to explain how men had influenced the lives of the three Garland sisters.

"We were all born," she began, "in a very small Midwestern town, Grand Rapids, Minn.—not Michigan, but Minnesota. Sue, the oldest, was born in 1915. I was born in 1917, and Judy in 1922.

"My dad was a vaudevillian. His name was Frank Gumm. My mother, Ethel, was playing piano in the pit of a theater in Marquette, Mich., when she met Dad. They formed a Vaudeville act called Jack and Virginia Lee—Sweet Southern Singers.

"When they got married, and Mother got pregnant with Sue, my dad, who was a very wonderful and enterprising man, decided that they had better stop traveling. His one big financial asset in life was a large diamond ring. That's all he really had to his name.

"One evening when he and mother hit Grand Rapids, Minn., he gave his diamond ring as a down payment on a small movie theater. This was back in the days of silent movies, and Mama used to play the piano in the pit while Daddy projected the films."

Readers in the Front Row

"When we three girls were born, we used to sit in the front row, and that's how we really learned to read, because of the titles. Mama wanted the three of us to sit in the front row so that she could keep an eye on us while she was playing the piano.

"On Saturdays Sue and I would go on stage as an extra added attraction and sing duets. Then when Judy was three, Dad let her sing 'Jingle Bells.' She was such a ham she wouldn't get off. Dad had to come from the wings and carry her off.

"We lived a terribly normal existence—none of the born-in-a-trunk bit. We lived in a real nice two-story house in Grand Rapids, right on the corner across the street from the grade school. We were one happy family. Dad taught us to be grateful for what we had."

When Virginia was 8 her parents found the winters in Minnesota too rigorous and just for a change took a trip to southern California. "All of us went," Virginia recalls, "and we were so taken by the climate that Dad drove back to Grand Rapids, sold the theater and moved us to Los Angeles—with no prospects of any kind.

"When we got to Los Angeles, we lived first in a house in Glendale. Then somebody told my father about a little theater for sale in Lancaster, a city north of Los Angeles in the Mojave Desert. The man who owned the theater ran it himself. He sold the tickets, collected the tickets, then ran back and started the film. Dad bought the theater, and we lived in Lancaster for seven years. Mama played the piano and taught us girls how to sing. She let us sing in the theater on weekends and then on one other day, she would drive us 60 miles to Los Angeles where we appeared on a kiddy program over Station KFWB.

"The guy who emceed the program was later fired for saying into the microphone when he thought he was off the air, 'Well, that should hold the little so-and-sos!'

"Judy, Sue and I earned our first money, $10 a week, singing at Loew's State during Christmas. They would only let us sing in the chorus. They didn't think we were good enough for anything else.

"Gradually we got better and started singing around Los Angeles and Long Beach, which we all loved because we got to go to the beach and take the rides on the amusement pier. In 1934, just as a lark, Mother took us to Chicago, where we worked the World's Fair. We worked at a place called Old Mexico and were billed as the Gumm Sisters."

Stint at Old Mexico

"We worked, not because we needed the money, but because we wanted to. I remember Dad didn't want us to go to Chicago. He was against it, but when Mother said okay, he gave her $500 worth of traveler's checks, but she was determined not to use them. Anyway, Old Mexico folded, and we got a job at the Oriental Theater in Chicago. The M.C. was George Jessel. Somehow he thought we were a comedy act. 'I can't introduce you as the Gumm Sisters,' he told us. 'It sounds too ridiculous.' Mama asked him what we should change it to. Jessel said he didn't know but would think of something before the second show. We were standing in the wings waiting to go on, when he motioned and introduced us as the Garland Sisters. Sue was then 19. I was 17, and Judy was 12 and perfectly normal.

"Until then the only man in our lives was our father. We loved and respected him. He was a kind man, a responsible man, an enterprising man. He showed us love and affection, and whatever happened to us afterward—no one can blame him. He died of a heart attack when he was 49."

One summer when the Garland Sisters were playing Lake Tahoe, Sue fell in love with a musician named Lee Cahn. Her parents tried to dissuade her from marriage, but at 20 Sue felt entitled to make her own decision. The marriage lasted six years. It was childless. Two years later Sue Garland married another musician, a trumpet player in the Artie Shaw Band, Jack Cathcart, now musical director at the Riviera Hotel in Las Vegas.

This past May, after she had obtained a divorce so that her bandleader husband might marry a younger girl, Sue Garland, 49, was found dead in her Las Vegas home. She had previously attempted suicide by taking near-fatal doses of Nembutal. This time the dose was fatal.

Of this tragedy, all Virginia Thompson will say is: "It was a sordid domestic mess. Living in Las Vegas, that's not a particularly tranquil atmosphere—the gambling, the girls, the temptations. When Jack and Sue obtained a divorce—that was the end for her. She went the sleeping pills route. Somehow the Garland females can't stand the loss of love.

"After Daddy died and Judy turned against her, Mama also tried suicide. Judy has tried it over and over again. I'm the only one who hasn't. I think it's because I'm happily married.

"What loused Judy up, I'm convinced, is psychiatry. She was the most happy, normal, lively, laughing girl you ever met until she began going to a psychiatrist. This was when she was a teenager at M-G-M after they'd signed her at $125 a week to begin with. Of course when she began going to the headshrinker she was earning big money. The first time she went into analysis, she stayed for 3 years, at $20 an hour, 5 days a week.

"How she started the psychiatrist bit is absolutely fantastic. As I remember, she was very much in love at the time with a writer-director. One day the three of us were sitting in a restaurant and Judy concocted a story about going up in a parachute ride with Mickey Rooney at an amusement park and getting stuck. The story was pure fiction—Judy liked to concoct these stories—she was always imaginative and creative—but the writer-director told her she was a pathological liar and he recommended she go to a psychiatrist.

"Judy was so much in love with him, his every word was a command. Well, after the psychiatrist got through with Judy, he convinced her that her family was no good for her. Mother used to handle Judy's finances. She bought her some wonderful annuity insurance—it was expensive—but Judy could have retired at age 30 independently wealthy. When she got through with the psychiatrist, she canned Mama and got a business manager who cashed in the policies, and after that it was one financial mess after another for her.

"Mama never took a dime from Judy. After Judy got divorced from David Rose and then married Vincente Minnelli, we all broke apart. Mama came to live in Dallas and managed a theater for a time, but then Judy tried to cut her throat and Mama raced back to Hollywood to help. She never did come back to Dallas. Sad—she could've had a nice life here. Instead, she stayed out there, and Ida Koverman, she was L. B. Mayer's secretary, got her a job working in an aircraft factory. One day when Mama was broke, Ida said to her, 'Now listen, this is just ridiculous. You've spent a fortune on Judy. She owes you something.' By then Judy was married to Sid Luft. She and Sid were down at the Philharmonic. So Mama went down to see Judy backstage. But Judy wouldn't see her. She sent Sid out to talk to her, but the conversation ended in nothing. Mama just left and she never took a penny from Judy."

Blames the Men in Her Life

"Later, Mama tried suicide and several years later, she died. But I don't blame Judy, I blame the men in her life, men she's been unable to cope with, ambitious men, complex men, driving men. Judy is no beauty. She was never any beauty. I guess in a theatrical world of great beauty, she felt inferior. She has always demanded love for reassurance, and I guess she's had to buy it.

"If only she had married a doctor, a lawyer, someone not in show business, someone who was not dependent on her for money, someone with integrity and achievement who could love her for herself and not her fame, she might have been all right. But now I'm afraid she's lost.

"I was a singer with bands. I worked with Kay Thompson and her group. I worked at M-G-M. I played all the large cities. But I was not infected by the so-called big time. I was able to move to Dallas, to adjust, to lower the tempo of my life, to sit and think and develop a sensible set of values. I know what's important and what is not.

"I pray to God that it's not too late for Judy, that somehow, somewhere, someday she can settle down with a plain, decent, self-respecting man. Money cannot buy her love, friendship, health or happiness. She still has her voice, and she still has her children. I pray she keeps them, because once they're gone—I'm just afraid to say what I think. Oh, I'm so afraid."

Pictures of Judy

"I met these stars, and I had to have pictures of them. I bought a Brownie Starflash. I'd go to the hotels where they were staying and I'd call them up on the house phones and say, 'Hello, Miss Garland, this is a fan of yours and I'd like to know when you are coming down so I can get your autograph.' And she'd say, 'Oh, about nine o'clock.' And she'd come down at eleven. She was always late."

—paparazzo Tony Rizzo

Offstage

Judy was still sleeping. I sat on the bed beside her and gently shook her shoulder. She wrapped her arms around me. "Don't ever leave me, Johnny," she whispered.

"Hey Judy, listen—I've got a party for us. It'll be fun." I watched her lips part slowly, but she didn't say anything. A thin string of saliva bridged the corner of her mouth. She's doped up, I told myself. I rubbed my knuckles into the back of her neck.

"How many Seconal did you take, Judy?"

"Mmm . . . couple."

Damn, I thought disgustedly, this'll throw off all my timing. I'd plotted our sleep schedule carefully to allow for a week of TV appearances. If I let Judy sleep now, on Saturday night, she'd be up all day Sunday, all Sunday night, a nervous wreck by Monday. And I'd be a wreck with her. The only thing to do was get her up.

I brought her ear to my mouth. "Where's the Ritalin, honey?"

"Mmm . . . pillbox."

I rummaged through Judy's purse and found the pillbox. It was empty. I left the bed and roamed the suite, looking for just a few grams of Ritalin. Nothing. I could not find one solitary tablet, not in the bathroom, not on the night table, not on the dresser, not on top of the TV set—and not on the floor, I discovered, brought finally to my knees to

peer under both beds, praying to spot a couple of the tiny, slate gray specks on the carpet.

We were out of Ritalin. I glanced at the telephone. It would be impossible to track down one of Judy's doctors at ten o'clock on a Saturday night.

And then I remembered: two blocks from the Hilton was the Park Sheraton Hotel, with a pharmacy that kept Judy's prescription on file. I was sure I could fast-talk them out of twenty pills.

I shrugged into my coat, Judy was sleeping like a contented koala, breathing regularly. And all is turmoil about her, I thought.

The block between Sixth and Seventh avenues is the longest in the city. I cursed my way through the half-frozen puddles, my hands jammed deep into my pockets, my neck pulled into my collar. I watched my breath make little puffs of steam between the snowflakes.

Fortunately, I had no trouble at the Park Sheraton. They gave me the prescription. As I stood in line at the cashier, waiting to pay, I grabbed a pack of pocket Kleenex from the counter and tore it open. My nose had started to run.

Back at Judy's bedside, I slipped her four tablets. Did you ever try giving pills to a sleeping woman? It's not easy. You have to hold her head upright with one hand, and tilt the glass to her lips with the other, and pinch her Adam's apple, and wipe the excess water from her chin, and push a wastepaper basket against her chest when she starts to retch.

Eventually I got the pills down Judy's esophagus and retired to the adjoining room to read the Sunday *Times,* which I'd bought at the Hilton newsstand. I figured the pills would take effect in half an hour or so and we could meet Linda at the party.

I picked up tomorrow's Arts & Leisure section.

Thirty minutes later I finished the theater news and was about to start on the Book Review when I glanced at Judy, lying in the next room, still motionless, still drugged. I crossed into the bedroom and once more shook her by the shoulder.

"Come on, Judy, let's go, rise and shine."

Judy was still in a stupor. Nothing made any sense to the dull and vacant pupils she turned on me. "Judy, come *on,*" I said, a little more urgently, "we're going to a party."

"Mmm . . . you go . . ." she said, her lids closing again. I felt a sudden surge of resentment. Okay, fuck it, I thought angrily, stay here, sleep all week, throw all the work and planning down the toilet, I don't care. I'm going to this party with or without you. Enough of this shit.

All right, I told myself, softening somewhat, I'd give Judy another quarter hour, and if she didn't show signs of animation by then, I'd leave and meet Linda alone.

I went back to the living room couch and opened the Book Review. Some trout fisherman in Ketchum, Idaho, had been an intimate of Hemingway's and his reminiscences were critiqued on the front page. Ernest had been a great outdoorsman, knew how to cast his trout line, never killed an animal unnecessarily, yeah yeah yeah, the usual Hemingway bullshit.

But halfway down the page the review quoted a remark the guy had heard from the famous author. It was in relation to the fine, true experience of shooting zebras or some such, but Hemingway had said, Remember, once you have the memory of an experience, no one can take it away from you.

I looked at Judy, asleep just twenty feet away from me. Something made me rise, and—marking my place in the article with my finger—walk slowly to her bedside. I stood there, gazing down at her recumbent, quietly breathing form, and suddenly the tragedy of it welled into my throat with a choking gush, and I found myself fighting to blink back simultaneous terror and pity.

I swallowed rapidly, twice, three times. Yes, I thought, Hemingway is right, once you have the memory of something it's yours forever, and my mind, as if spun into reverse by the press of a projector button, was instantly reviewing the hundreds of fine and hideous things Judy and I had been through together: the food fight at Larry's, Mr. Lee's hat, the hospital fuck, playing poker, carrying her over the Fenway threshold, dancing at the Shelton Towers . . . and the songs, oh, Christ, the wonderful singing, the way she'd lasered into me with her voice, the way she'd made something vital out of dead words and music, yes, it seemed to me my songs had been dead before I brought them to her, and she'd borne them, given them birth, given them life from the womb of her mouth, and nobody could take that from me, no one could erase my memories, even this one now, remembering it as it happened, fixing in my mind forever the image of my own tears, dropping helplessly on the blanket, nobody could ever take that from me, no, nobody . . . ever . . .

And I knew then, through this clanging, irreversible feeling, that hope was over . . . that Judy and I could never make it together.

I fell on the bed and pressed my face into the hollow of her side, just above the hip, and shook with a barrage of great, wracking sobs I'd never known I was capable of before Judy.

This woke her. At least to the point of semiconsciousness. "Wh . . . what is it . . . why are you crying . . . ?"

"Oh, Judy . . ." It was difficult to speak with my nose full of tears and a mouth contorted with anguish. "You just do it to yourself, every time . . . and there's no way to fight it . . . it's inside you, it's inside you, and I can't help you . . . it's inside you . . ."

She was beneath comprehension. "Wh . . . what's inside me?"

"You just make it impossible . . . for anyone to help you . . . because you won't let them . . . something inside you defeats you . . . and destroys you . . ."

I was blabbering like an infant, feeling the moisture running from my nostrils down over my upper lip. I kept shaking my head and blubbering. I stumbled to my feet and jerked a length of toilet paper from the roll in the bathroom, enough to blow my nose on.

"Johnny . . ." Judy said, "don't you love me?"

"Of course I love you!" I threw myself violently back upon her. "That's why I'm crying, you jerk, because I love you and I can't help you . . . *no-body* can . . . it's inside you, and you're the only one who can do something about it . . . but you won't . . . you can't . . ."

I sat on Judy's bed and breathed in as many deep gulps of air as I could, sniffing back the phlegm. I had to stop this sobbing. I felt completely drained. I sat there for perhaps a minute, watching Judy's eyes slip from incomprehension to rationality and back again. She lay, inert, on the pillow. I could see she'd be asleep again soon.

"All right, look . . ." I said weakly; even to speak was an effort. "I'm gonna go to this party . . . I'll give you a call later . . ."

I got up, went into the living room, and put on my coat. As I left the suite, Judy was lying on her right side, facing the window. The eye I could see was open, but I knew it would close again within a few seconds.

As the door clicked and shut behind me, I wondered whether Judy realized what had just happened.

Bernard Weinraub

FROM *THE NEW YORK TIMES*   JUNE 27, 1969

Thousands Wait for Last Good-by to Judy Garland

Her fans said good-by to Judy Garland yesterday.

They arrived before dawn at the Frank E. Campbell Funeral Home and stood for hours behind police barricades—thousands of elderly women, weeping young men, teenaged girls, housewives, nuns, priests, beggars, cripples and hippies.

They packed 81st Street between Madison and Fifth Avenues, streaming into the funeral to gaze into the glass-enclosed coffin containing the body of the 47-year-old singer who, in death as well as in life, stirred emotions in her fans.

They wept.

"People identified with that woman," Mrs. Marilyn Ford, a 23-year-old Queens housewife, said as she stepped out of the funeral home. "Everyone's got sadness and problems, everyone gets lonely. Judy Garland made all of us feel something tied her and us together."

Flowers From Many

Through the gray, murky afternoon, nearly 5,000 fans waited patiently in line, some for two hours, to walk into the chapel.

Inside, the fragrance of flowers suffused the air—bouquets and wreaths of roses and pink and white carnations and yellow spider mums—flowers sent by Fred Astaire, James Stewart, Sargent Shriver, William Paley, Irving Berlin and dozens of other friends and fans.

A dozen feet from the steel coffin of white and gold stood a big wreath of peonies shaped like a rainbow—for Miss Garland's most famous song, "Over the Rainbow." The wreath was signed simply: "Cathy, Lou, Mike, Maria, Pam."

"She's found that rainbow now," Mrs. Mary Roberts, a 20-year-old typist, said quietly after staring for a moment at the coffin, which was lined with pale blue velvet. "I hope she's finally got some peace."

By early evening, nearly 10,000 persons had walked past the coffin. The line, eight abreast, curled around 81st Street to Fifth Avenue, then along the avenue to 82nd Street between Fifth and Madison Avenues. There was a four-hour wait to enter the funeral home.

Crowds Expected

"I don't remember anything of this magnitude and I go back 20 years," said Ted Thorne, vice president of Frank E. Campbell. "We sort of anticipated it."

Most of the funeral arrangements were made by Miss Garland's daughter, Liza Minnelli, the actress-singer, who remained in seclusion through the day.

Miss Garland's fifth husband, Mickey Deans, a discotheque manager, visited the funeral home in the morning and afternoon. He conferred there with family friends on burial arrangements.

Mr. Deans appeared haggard. He wore dark glasses and nervously ran his fingers through unruly black hair. His black, tapered pants were rumpled, barely touching his ankle-length boots.

"I still can't believe it," he said hoarsely.

Mr. Deans and family friends delayed the start of the public viewing for more than an hour—from 11 A.M. to noon—to allow cosmeticians further time.

Miss Garland's slight, frail body was clothed in the high-necked gray chiffon gown in which she had been married in March. Silver slippers with silver buckles were on her feet. Her hands covered a prayer book that rested near the gown's gold and pearl belt. She wore a triple strand wedding ring on the little finger of her right hand.

As visitors streamed slowly into the chapel—designed vaguely in the style of a New England church—many placed carnations and daisies on the pews. Many men carried single roses.

"She was too sensitive and vulnerable to life, and it got to her," said Dennis Beattie, a thin, solemn, 28-year-old waiter. "She appealed to all the people who were sensitive and vulnerable."

There were large numbers of Negro women, too, young and middle-aged.

"Judy gave love and you got the feeling there wasn't an ounce of hate in her," whispered Mrs. Helen McClean Jaafer, a Manhattan housewife. "There's so much hatred now, so much meanness, and I think Judy Garland was just too kind for this kind of world."

Minister Flies Here

The body arrived early yesterday in New York from London, where the singer and actress died Sunday, apparently of an accidental overdose of sleeping pills. Mr. Deans and the Rev. Peter Delaney, who married the couple, accompanied the body.

A hearse then took the coffin to the funeral home, where the public viewed the body until late last night. The public may also view the coffin from 8 A.M. to 11 A.M. today.

Mr. Delaney will officiate at today's private funeral services, starting at 1 P.M. in the chapel. James Mason, who starred with Miss Garland in *A Star Is Born*, will deliver the eulogy.

Among those invited to the funeral services—from which the press and public are barred—are Mayor Lindsay, Richard Avedon, the photographer, and such performers as Frank Sinatra, Cary Grant, Lauren Bacall, June Allyson, Katharine Hepburn, Mickey Rooney, Sammy Davis Jr., Bobby Short and Sid Caesar.

Interment will take place at Ferncliff Cemetery in Hartsdale, N.Y. Family friends said that the body would be placed in a crypt until a mausoleum was built.

Lorna Remembers

"The only sad thing is that she ended up so far away from all of us, with a husband she hardly knew. It was all Mickey Deans's idea to have the open casket. Mama wanted to be cremated. She would have hated all those people staring at her."

—Lorna Luft to Rex Reed, 1972

Barbara Grizzuti Harrison

FROM *McCALL'S*   MAY 1975

Liza Talks

The headlines announce that the Los Angeles Police Department is preparing for imminent food riots. But as one is driven from the merciless squalor and razzmatazz tackiness of downtown L.A. to the subtropical opulence and preternatural stillness of Beverly Hills, food riots seem like a figment of a malevolent idiot's imagination. The taxi driver talks briefly about food riots, and then, as if to push the specter of that evil day away, asks me what I am doing here: I'm here to interview Liza Minnelli. After a few puzzled seconds, he says, "Oh—the one with the funny hair. Judy Garland's daughter." Pointing up to the hills where Liza and the Never-Never-Land people live, he says: "These people don't know how to live—only how to die."

According to film people, Liza Minnelli, the Superstar who has won a Tony award, an Emmy and an Oscar, is one of the few "bankable" female movie stars; like Barbra Streisand, her name alone guarantees that the several million dollars needed to finance a movie can be raised. Yet for many people Liza is still—and always will be—Judy Garland's daughter. And because she is her mother's daughter, many people, unable to divorce her from the image of Judy that has been imprinted on their minds, are bound to think of Liza as having a talent for dying—a thrust toward death rather than a gift for life.

Before I left New York to interview Liza, I had collected a portfolio of she's-just-like-her-mama stories. But, strangely, even the people merchandising the most vicious and slanderous stories sounded the same admonishment: "Be kind to her. Protect her." After taking enormous relish in describing a dippy decadent, a frenetic pleasure-seeker whose appetite for gobbling up experience of every variety would make the stomach of a confirmed hedonist lurch, all the people who knew people who know Liza added, "She's nice."

Just before I left New York I read this tidbit in *Women's Wear Daily:* "Liza Minnelli's steady date in Paris is no longer the Baron de Rede, but she is with a gang of Brazilian transvestite dancers." The same day (talk about contradictions), a hardened show-biz professional told me, with unmistakable conviction and sincerity, the kind of sentimental story press agents dream up for Doris-Day-girl-next-door movie actresses: Liza harbors waifs. She collects stray animals. And when Liza takes on a stray, she really takes it on. Liza, her friends say, is not prone to self-gratifying, impulsive bursts of sentiment that, when they threaten to inconvenience her, she promptly forgets. If one is gathered to her ample bosom, one *stays* gathered. Just as, friends say, when Liza, then 21, married her first husband—musician Peter Allen—she took on responsibility for Peter's mother and sister . . . and just as, when Liza dated Desi Arnaz, Jr., she made it her business to see that Desi and his mother, Lucille Ball, were reconciled. Just as Liza, only 23, made all the arrangements for Judy's funeral single-handedly, never once giving way to either self-aggrandizing public heroics or to hysteria. And, friends say, Liza mothers her half sister and her half brother, Lorna and Joey Luft, pushing Lorna's career along, seemingly unafflicted with sibling rivalry or the fear endemic in superstars that their own birthright will be eclipsed.

Liza, her friends say, ends every conversation with a question: "Do you love me? Do you really love me?"

So. What do we have here? Waif posing as decadent? Decadent posing as waif? Waif searching for Mama? Or earth mother searching for waifs?

And how, in Hollywood, land of the dream factory, can the real Liza Minnelli be found?

My first meeting with Liza: The door to my hotel room is flung open. On the threshold is a slim, wan young woman, huge brown eyes bleary but alight with curiosity. I am the object of Liza's curiosity. Already—immediately—by some strange alchemy, my objectivity has begun to wilt at the edges. The big eyes are vulnerable. Liza throws her arms around me in a bear hug: "Hi, honey," she says, echoes of the Judy tremor in her nervous giggle. She flops on my bed. She gulps down a bullshot (vodka and bouillon), says she hates interviews, hates "plastic New York people." I am given to understand that she exempts me from that category: "They told me you were a nice lady," Liza says. (*Nice* is a word Liza uses a lot.) We talk, with no opening gambits, no delicate probing, preliminary explorations, as if we were picking up the threads of a conversation we've been having for years. Somehow, I find myself telling Liza my life; and Liza listens as if it were the most interesting story she had ever heard . . . Is Liza throwing up a smoke screen to disarm me, to force me to like her so that I will be too embarrassed to ask the difficult questions I am here to ask her? She is, after all, a consummate actress. My journalist's mind pushes all the buttons while Liza Minnelli, Superstar, talks to me and listens to me as if I am to be trusted. I push the buttons called Cynicism, Skepticism. The buttons are inoperative . . . within 15 minutes, I hear myself ask, "Liza, do you like me? Do you really like me?"

Back only four days from a series of one-night stands in Europe, married only 21 weeks to producer Jack Haley, Jr., Liza is exhausted. She talks—streams of consciousness: "So tired, honey . . . I've had fittings all day, suicide time, I hate fittings . . . Why does everyone write about me as if I'm a Ping-Pong ball? Why does everyone think I'm frantic? I have friends, I'm busy, but I'm not *crazy*! I'm a private person; I don't give a damn about what people have written about me; half the things I read are lies. They don't want me to be good or happy—they want me to be *Interesting*. They'd like me to be weird. They all want to hit pay dirt. *Dirt*. Once I said to an interviewer, Look, I'm sorry I'm not a nut, but I'm not, so do you want to drop the story? Because I'm not going to sit here and pretend that I'm crazy to you, because I'm not. I'm healthy. I'm basically a very happy person. People like to trip me up on the fact that I bite my nails. Well, that's a habit, and if I'm biting my nails while I'm figuring out a great way to play a role, don't write it down for other people to read that I'm neurotic because I bite my nails. How can they judge me because I bite my nails? Does that invalidate everything I do and everything I am?

"I'm afraid of things; of course I'm afraid of things. When I'm on a plane, I look around at people's faces to see if they look like the faces of people who're gonna die. And I'm afraid of open spaces, of being exposed. Like when they ride off into the sunset on a horse in the movies? Ugh. I'd drop right off the horse. Dead. All that emptiness. Nothing to touch. When I wake up alone in a strange city and Jack's not in bed to hold on to, I get terrified. I'm frozen when I'm not with somebody I know and love.

"Does everybody feel that they're conning people, that someday everyone will find out that you're not as good as they think you are? Probably you never feel like that. You *do? Terrific!* You know, one day, when I was a kid—Queen of Ugly, that was me, brown oxfords and all—I was dancing on the lawn; I thought people would throw me pennies. And a car passed by and a woman leaned out of the window and vomited. *Ha!* How's that for rejection? Daddy laughed and told me it was all right, that it wasn't *me* who was making her vomit. It's nice to have someone take the hurt away. Daddy always did. You have to have a sense of humor to get out of this business alive. Like, they keep shoving rotten scripts down my throat, they think I'm gonna burn myself up, they want to chew me up and spit me out while I'm still going strong. Well, that's their problem. You get yourself out before you get killed. Mama found it hard to run for her life. When I was a kid, I'd find myself dragging her out of places, literally yanking her away and saying, Mama, you're leaving, you can't subject yourself to this. The rule is, Get out with your head on.

"Listen, when I don't like interviewers, I sit around and give stock answers and I become Liza's protector. I have every right to be Liza's protector. Every businessman in the world protects himself, every kid on the first day of school protects herself. When you're in the limelight and your business is exposing yourself—selling yourself (I'm a commodity. But I'm a commodity that gives people pleasure, that's okay.)—people feel cheated when they learn you protect yourself. But you're not building a case against me, are you? I like you. I want to be your friend. Are we friends?"

Reaching the limits of her exhaustion, Liza begins to tremble; her eyes tear, she goes to the bathroom and retches. "Oh, honey, I'm so sorry. Must have been something I picked up in Europe. Gotta go. Dinner at Chasen's with my husband. Gotta put on my professional face." She giggles. "You know, when I was a kid, I never believed the Queen peed. Well, the Queen pees. And Liza vomits."

As Liza walks down the hall, she yells back, "Hey, isn't it terrific? We're friends. You're a good lady. I'll get you into a better hotel tomorrow; this isn't good enough for you. And remember—it wasn't you who made me vomit."

She lives in a rambling house high on a hill in West Los Angeles. The reflected light from the swimming pool that overlooks the city dances on the cathedral ceiling of the living room. It is a warm, lived-in house that would win nobody's award for exquisite taste, not a house beautiful, but a house loved: mock-Spanish furniture; in the bedroom she shares with Haley a mock-Tudor four poster; a family room with—the only conspicuous sign of affluence—an antique billiard table; movie memorabilia everywhere (missing: a picture of her mama); on every surface plastic signs that one would not be surprised to find in the bedroom of a sweet 11-year-old girl: *I like your face. You make me happy.*

Hollywood-type servants—golden, oiled people who look as if they just dropped in to use the swimming pool—slip in and out performing various services. Her bags are unpacked. Vitamins are offered to her. A young woman who looks like a studio starlet tells Liza her eyelashes are in the silver tray in her "closet"—a room as large as a good-size suburban bedroom. A manservant watches me warily, reserving judgment, protecting his lady, offering me drinks tight-lipped.

We sit in the conversation pit with choreographer Ron Fields and Tom Mankiewicz, the screenwriter. Liza is digging an album cut by blues singer Etta James; with quivering intensity she listens to the sounds of a woman recently released from a drug bust. Liza's generosity spills over: "You've gotta love a lady who's come through like that. Can we give her a party? Can we help promote her? How can we help her?" Liza has never met Etta James; but she loves her because . . . "Oooh, just listen . . . you can hear all the pain and all the hurt, but she's gone beyond the pain, she's singing from where the bravery is." Liza turns to me, explaining: "Pain and hurt aren't art. They have to be transformed. You can't just offer people your pain; that's like masturbating in public. It's a no-no." Liza sings a plaintive little song for me, full of angst and sentiment: "Did you think that was good? *Wrong!* Here's the right way": and then Liza sings the same song, this time with a hint of wry self-mockery, a conscious bravado. She is superlative. "Terrif', huh? Give 'em your courage, not your pain. *Give* it to 'em." Suddenly I understand that it's not the eyelashes, the makeup, the Halston clothes that transform plain Liza into Superstar Liza; it is Liza's luminous determination to offer them her courage, to sock them with her *Yes!*

It is about her demons that one must question this lady, this woman who worships bravery above all other qualities, this glamorous superstar who is so obviously, so intimately, acquainted with pain.

Liza answers questions—even voyeuristic questions—with simplicity and the appearance of absolute candor. She has no clearly developed or articulated religious or political beliefs; a creature of instinct, she tends to play it all by ear; a child of the films, she tends more to anecdote and flashy visual image than to analysis. She is so much a product of the Hollywood dream factory that—to an interviewer's constant befuddlement—Liza will be discussing politics and suddenly Cyd Charisse will be wandering through her sentence. She will be talking about religion, and suddenly she will segue into a story about George Hamilton. It is as if Liza has no frame of reference other than the magic screen. And she frequently gets things mixed up: After laughing unguardedly at a rather rude joke, Liza told me that she had sworn never again to laugh at a Polish joke because, "I saw on 'The World at War' on TV about the Reds invading the ghetto at Warsaw [an event that has never occurred in the history of the world], and I decided it was too cruel." She got it all wrong but the essential fact—that people ought not to be cruel; it is a knack Liza has.

Her lack of formal education (one year at the Sorbonne, which Liza dismisses as being of no consequence) is a liability she seeks to compensate for in ways that are original, to say the least: Every week, for example, Liza and her husband and Fred Ebb (the lyricist who wrote *Cabaret,* put together her nightclub act and has been her musical mentor from the beginning) call one another from wherever they happen to be in the world, and Ebb and Haley teach Liza three new words to increase her vocabulary . . . which words Liza then writes on her left foot, in Magic Marker, to rehearse in bed that night. On her foot the day Liza offered it to me for inspection was the word *litigious.* Liza used it in a sentence: "Sid Luft [Judy's third husband and the father of Joey and Lorna]," she said, snarling, "is *litigious.*" It is in unguarded moments like this that Liza reveals her loves and fears and animosities: It is unlikely that she would have allowed herself to tell me directly that she disliked Luft, a fact her vicious snarl and her application of the pejorative to him made perfectly apparent. But her formal answers to formal questions are revealing, too—precisely because she has not developed coherent attitudes. The face she has prepared to greet the world is a slippery mask. It does not protect her very well.

So here—in guarded and unguarded moments—is Liza, a woman of contradictions, confusions and with her share of despair. And—I join the chorus—a *nice* woman.

Liza talks about drugs and sex: "I've heard all the rumors. I know they say I'm shooting up, pills—the whole works. *How dare they?* They're gonna try to grind me up. Well, I won't step into the grinder. They can make up a version of me—all I really am is an Italian broad—and put that version in their grinder. Look, here's the truth: I'm in Brazil, at a big party, right? And around comes this funny cigarette. I'd never tried it, and I said, Why not? Everybody else is doing it. I took a puff and nothing happened . . . three puffs, and I didn't think anything was happening. And then suddenly, oh, God, I saw everything and everybody that I didn't want to see. I've got such a huge imagination: I looked around and thought, What am I *doing* at this party? I didn't like the way the stuff smelled, the way it tasted. I wouldn't go near anything hallucinatory. I don't want to find out if there are serpents in my heart. I value my brain. I value life and I want to *see* it. And I'm not gonna do anything to mess it up.

"After I did *Cabaret,* everybody started talking about me—they got me mixed up with the role—as if I were a decadent femme fatale like Sally Bowles . . . who was as *fatale,* incidentally, as an after-dinner mint. [Parenthetically, it seems worth noting that the lyrics Ebb composes and arranges for Liza seem almost calculatedly designed to exploit the doom-ridden-like-mama mystique; he is her friend but also her merchandiser: He knows how to package a commodity.] Suddenly I'm reading that I'm dating people I've never even heard of. *Brazilian transvestite dancers?* They made it sound as if something sexual was going on with me and them. That stinks. In the first place, the dancers are gay. Oh, no, the whole thing is too ridiculous. They were a great group of dancers, an adorable bunch of people, and they weren't doing enough business in Paris. So I said, Look, why don't you use me? Give a special show and invite me, and we'll get a whole bunch of press people to come and it'll generate some excitement for you. Their show was *terrific.* It wasn't a drag show, really; they really weren't transvestites. I mean, a lot of guys dressed crazy. They were sort of saying, We're not men, we're not women, we're *people.* So I helped some terrific artists and the press turns it into *Liza's having an affair with Brazilian transvestites.* And the Baron de Rede was never my boyfriend; he's a friend of the Rothschilds, who are super good friends of mine, and we had *dinner* together for goodness sake. And how could I have a boyfriend? I'm *married!*"

Liza, who is well aware that like her mother before her she has a vast and adoring following among gay men, launches into what amounts to a stirring defense of heterosexual love and sexual fidelity. She is also aware that gossip mongers have placed her squarely in the middle of the swinging Andy Warhol androgynous bisexual set—a fact her words, if they are to be taken at face value (and, looking at her open, honest face, that's the way one would prefer to take them), belie:

"There's this poem: I don't know exactly how it goes, but it's something like, 'Men swear they live for beauty and art, but they really live for fashion.' In this day and age of everybody going out and doing things because they're the fashionable thing to do, there are just certain things that I don't think are right. Bisexuality is one of them. It takes away intimacy. It takes away having to deal on a one-to-one basis, which is so scary and so wonderful, which is what I thought it was all about. It's a cop-out. It's a way of saying, 'I don't love you, but I want to have sex, and if there's somebody else there, it's okay to have sex because then it's just a party.' I don't understand the choreography of group sex. I'm a romantic; I'd rather sleep by myself than have an orgy."

Liza, schlumping around in a blue bathrobe, looking about as decadent as Andy Hardy's girlfriend, pauses to answer the phone. It is her father, Vincente Minnelli. Her plain face lights up. "Oh, Daddy," Liza squeals, "I love you better than anybody in the world." She dances with glee. This is the girl people describe as a kinky sexual consumer? It's hard to believe.

On the other hand, there are things it's hard to add up, things that jangle, sentences that feel like overkill: Liza, who has generous words for practically everybody you've ever heard of in Hollywood, was vicious—aside from her fierce reference to Sid Luft—only twice in my presence. Once, when she asked her manservant for a record "that *faggot* has"—her voice hissing the term for the unidentified homosexual; and once, as we were stretched across her bed, watching a Fred Astaire movie: "Astaire," Liza said, "is the only elegant American actor we've ever had." She mentions that a famous actor, also noted for his elegance "is really British—and a— *faggot.*"

The word produces an automatic snarl. And yet Liza talks sympathetically about the homosexual men who were Judy's greatest fans (one might be forgiven for assuming that Liza's attitudes toward homosexuals and homosexuality are not so uncomplicated as they appear to be on the surface): "Homosexual men identified with Mama—that poor little frail bird who sat there looking so vulnerable and singing 'Somewhere Over the Rainbow.' *There must be a place for me,* that's what she was saying. There must be a place for me that's better than this. Gay men recognized themselves in that tiny little woman up there calling for a better world, a place where she would be happier, where people would understand. Mama had style, and they loved it. She had razor-blade, zap humor; and she could cut you off at the ankles. She could make you curl up and die and scream laughing at the same time, because it was all so funny—even when it was killing you. My attitude is different from hers. The first word I say onstage is *Yes!* God, I hope I'll never change. Promise me you'll hit me if I change?"

Talk about sex automatically brings Liza around to talk about her marriages. Peter Allen, her first husband, is now a successful entertainer on the gay nightclub circuit in New York. The marriage was an inspiration of Judy's. Liza will not discuss the sexual aspects of that marriage—"That's one of the demons, honey"—but she talks freely about the problems of competition between her and Peter: "Women's success embarrasses men; a woman's afraid he'll leave 'cause he's embarrassed. Marriage to Peter was miserable—*horrible*. When we got married we were equal in terms of career success, and I went up and he went down. He almost broke up when I started making it big. And the minute I left he started writing marvelous songs. The competition nearly killed us both. That's why I always said, after Peter, that I'd never marry another actor, ever, ever . . . It was all nonsense about my marrying Peter Sellers . . . I'm married to the most wonderful man. He's so strong. *Totally male,* and always has been. Jack is very big— he's like a corner I can hide in. And he's kind. When I was little, I used to hear about the way he was always going out with some terrific-looking lady—he's a lot older than me—and he had this snappy reputation. I never dreamed he'd even look at me. What would a talented playboy want with me? And then I met him—and he was so *nice.* I said, 'Hey, you've got a pretty hot reputation.' He said, 'So do you. Have you done all the things they say you've done?' 'Nope,' I said. 'Neither have I,' he said. Jack and I don't compete. He knows I'm scared that my success will send the men I love running away, and once he said this terrific thing to me: He said, 'Do you know, if somebody ever said to me, Mr. Minnelli, could I have your autograph, I'd sign *Vincente* and be proud.' Isn't that gorgeous?"

While I am wondering whether Liza has made a Freudian slip—Vincente is her *father's* name, could Jack have said that?—Haley, dapper, handsome, walks in. Liza shrugs her small frame into his large body. There is a Doris Day/Rock Hudson scene complete with Liza making moues and singing snatches of songs into Haley's ear. They nuzzle each other's toes. I have heard it bruited about that Liza's is a marriage of convenience. If that is so, I am watching the best parody of domesticity ever produced.

Haley confirms Liza's estimate of him as a snapping wit and a marvelous raconteur. But an odd thing happens in the hour and a half that I spend with Liza and her husband: Liza calls Jack *Vincente* once; she calls him *daddy* twice. Haley looks at me to see if it's registered. I remember something a New York friend has said about Liza: "Liza's forced herself to believe that Vincente was always there for her. In fact, he was an absentee father. But she can't accept that. She denies it to herself. When you interview her, you'll hear her say, Daddy always took the hurt away. She won't be lying to you; she'll be lying to herself."

Does Liza lie to herself? Certainly her determined optimism frequently sounds like the bravado of a kid whistling past the graveyard. Liza doesn't want to know about the "serpents in her heart." Liza wants her demons "on the other side of the street." Liza says, "I believe in God. I believe in the tooth fairy. And I want to go to heaven. I'm sure there must be a heaven. I think nice people should be rewarded." Liza doesn't believe in analysis; she's into self-help: "I have a friend—*me*. I know more people in this town who spend their lives fooling analysts. Me, I'd rather cook something [Liza dumps a pile of cookbooks in my lap, promises to cook me fettucini Alfredo], take a drive or talk to somebody who's *up*. I'm not a moaner and groaner. Well, once I called my godmother, Kay Thompson, when I was depressed, and I howled, and she said, Why don't you learn to play the violin? And I said, What a terrific idea! She was saying, Why don't you take your mind off yourself, pal, it's not all that important . . . I don't believe in sitting out something that's painful and uncomfortable, it's just not where I want to be. I'd rather go to Disneyland . . . Look, aren't we lucky? All those people who say nasty things about me, think what pain they're in. And we're sitting here having a wonderful time. Here you are, phobic about flying, and you made it out here to see me—I'm so *honored*—and you made a new friend. And *I* made a new friend. Test me. I'm a sticker. I refuse to be one of the disappointments in your life.

"Look, I'm glad I'm an American. I'm glad I'm a girl. I'm glad I'm me. I like the way God made us. I like the things that happen to me. Little things, like having my cigarettes lit, like having doors opened for me. Big things: I like it that I worked so hard, that I can make people happy. I like it that something in my nature creates the desire always to be better—to be *good*.

"Hey, I'll tell you a terrific story: Once, when we were kids, we were all out with Mama at the Kennedy compound in Hyannis Port, and one of the

Kennedy kids said to my brother, *Do you know the Declaration of Independence?* 'No.' *Do you know the Gettysburg Address?* 'No.' Then Mama nudged Joey and he said to the Kennedy kid, *Can you whistle the overture to West Side Story?* . . . See, Mama used to settle all her political arguments by saying 'I'll call the President.' And Jack would always answer her calls. They'd call each other every Sunday . . . and he'd ask her to sing the last eight bars of 'Somewhere Over the Rainbow.'

"So what could be bad? I'm not afraid of growing old. I don't have the kind of face that'll fall apart. Beauty's never been the thing that I've been about, it's what's inside. Besides, I'm not gonna stay in this business forever. As soon as you're a success, you have to wean yourself away from it. I'd like to work with kids: There's this wonderful doctor—Glenn Doman— who works with brain-damaged kids at the Institute for the Achievement of Human Potential in Philadelphia. He won't accept defeat. It's like he refuses to believe in blindness or deafness. I honor him. Every human life can be redeemed, can be *orderly*. People *do* overcome. I'm so inspired by being alive. I want everybody to feel that way."

That's Liza's *Yes* with a vengeance. But there is another Liza. The Liza who says, "Women get old, they lose their beauty and then they're nothing, they're thrown out into the streets for garbage. Poets and statesmen are revered when they get old—but a *woman?*" The Liza who says: "I'd have been dead a long time ago if I hadn't been self-preservative. You have to say when it's enough. *Basta!*" The Liza who says, "It's hard, hard getting through life, but you've gotta, you just can't cave in, you've gotta keep going—you can't give way to despair." The Liza who says: "You can get lost wandering through the labyrinths of all the roles you put on—wife, actress—you can get scared trying to find the real person." The Liza who talks about her anxiety attacks: "My hands get ice-cold, I have palpitations. I become so aware that the machine—the body—is so vulnerable that it can just *stop*. I try to get up and put on a record and dance or do something. I find if I can name it it's much better: I tell myself I'm having an attack, a willy, a frazzly. I hate it. I say to myself, You are *not* going to have a heart attack and you are perfectly all right and don't be so silly. There comes a point when you're past being able to do something about it, and that's when real panic sets in . . . Don't ever joke about loonies. Madness is a dark pit."

It seems unfair to ask this Liza the mama-questions, unfair and unkind. But Liza, as usual, seeks to reassure: "Look, it's your job. I know you have to do it. We're finding out about each other, right? I could look at you and say, You're conning me by telling all about yourself so I'll spill to you and tell you all about myself. But I trust you. I won't allow myself to believe you're not good."

So Liza talks about Judy:

"She was proud of me. All I ever wanted was to be good. And that's what she wanted. I loved her in so many ways. She was a friend of mine—a trying friend, but a friend. She never treated me like a kid. I loved that. My English nanny treated me like a kid—she beat the hell out of me. And my daddy treated me like I was a princess. I had a crash course in growing up. I learned a lot too fast and then I had to sort it out. Too much, too fast, too soon. The circuits got overcharged. But Mama was always there for me. And Daddy was always there for me. They always told me I was wonderful. Always—from when I was a teeny tiny little girl, the Queen of Ug . . . Oh, I've said so many times how much I loved my mother, still love her. When she died, I wrote an article about her, about her humor and her love of life; the *Times* rejected it. They put in all the boring, maudlin, garbage stuff instead—dredged it all up. *Why?*"

"Do I have to talk about her any more? I don't know what else to say. Can't people accept that? How can they argue with that? Why do they want me to be the keeper of the flame and the destroyer of the myth at the same time? People are wishing things on me. It never crossed my mind that I would grow up to 'be' my mother till people told me so and made me afraid of it. I'm *me*. I've made it on my own.

"Of course it wasn't easy being Judy's kid. The pressure was tremendous. We traveled so much; I was never a normal kid. But Mama had such a sense of humor; and Daddy was so kind. Mama was always there. Say that. Say *Mama was always there*. I got a tremendous amount of love from both of them . . . and a tremendous amount of garbage. It was—how can I say?—crazy. But basically sane. Like, before Mama would do something she knew would drive me crazy, she'd warn me: 'Watch this,' she'd say. 'I'm gonna have to do something crazy.'

"I ignore everything that's ever written about her. They tried to take her away from me when she was alive, and they're still trying. It's just a continuation of the same old—.

"Nobody's had a happy childhood. Hey, it was really reassuring to me when I found that out. I'm not a freak. Everything became exaggerated because it was Judy doing it. Every mother has yelled at her kid. I'm not an exception. I'm not an *experiment*. Okay, I hate it when people shout and yell, so what? I am *not* the only kid that's been yelled at. This is what I tell myself: She did everything she ever wanted to do, including those suicide attempts. She never really denied herself anything for me. See, I say, she had a wonderful life—she did what she wanted to do. And I have no right to change her fulfillment into my misery. I'm on my own broom now.

"And about those suicide attempts. Those were just silly things to at-tract attention. She wouldn't have really done it in a million years. She'd come in and take two pills and say, *Ooooh, I can't take it anymore*. It was hys-teria—no, it was acting. *But she did not kill herself*. She died with dignity. Her body just gave out on her. She did things well. She died at the right time. She died when she was still able to work; she would have hated not being able to work. She didn't die of an overdose or any of that crap. She just passed away, joined the choir, took a taxi, however you want to put it. She did it with style. And I miss her terribly. We were always together. I know how she was and none of the bone pickers can take her away from me. I will not let them hurt me."

Liza has worn herself out. She gulps down a bullshot and says she thinks the "willies" are coming on. Her solution: "I'll sing for you. I'll sing 'It Was a Good Time.' I won't do it schmaltzy, I won't be maudlin. If I use my own pain, I'll bore myself to death. I'm not gonna mess people's heads up with my own private demons. So what I do is, I imagine somebody else's pain; I invent a little girl who hurts a lot and a mama who hurts a lot . . . and a daddy who's deserted them.

"The song starts with nursery rhymes . . .

"*Here we go round the mulberry bush* . . . I think of a woman who has a three-year-old daughter and the woman and the kid and her daddy are on a picnic and they're happy . . .

"*Mama wakes up and she's alone* . . . So I imagine this woman who's being abandoned by her husband; it's the first time she wakes up alone with nobody to touch, nobody to hold on to . . .

"*London Bridge is falling down* . . . She has to tell the kid, see, and she's trying so hard to hold on to him, and they're screaming and fighting, and she has to tell the kid there's no more *us* . . .

"*Mama will stay near you, not your dad, that's too bad* . . . Mama always stayed with the kid, she did it with dignity . . .

"*Daddy's gone a-hunting* . . . He's *gone!*"

Liza sings. On the words *Mama will stay near you, not your dad, that's too bad,* her voice catches and breaks and snarls. She is magnificent. She is suddenly beautiful and magic. She makes my flesh crawl.

And she believes—she truly believes—she is not singing about her own pain.

When the song is over, Liza, depleted, throws her arms around me. There is a giggle, a sob and an apology: "Sorry. It's such hard work. But the willies are going now."

Before I leave, I say to Liza, "Liza, I'm going to tell people I loved you. And they're all going to say you conned me."

"Don't give them a chance," Liza says. "Don't tell bad people. Don't ever give them a chance to take anything away from you."

Her final words, as she sees me off, are, "I'm not going to stop believing that people are good. I believe. I want to believe."

Kay Thompson, Liza's godmother, has said of her, "Liza always makes the right mistakes. She goes just so far and then she pulls back from the abyss." And what one wishes for Liza—who is a seeker after goodness, not a seeker after pleasure—is that the abyss will not yawn, that she will have bounty and safety and happiness . . . because she's *nice.*

Paul Rosenfield

FROM *THE LOS ANGELES TIMES*   MARCH 7, 1982

Lorna Luft's Road Gets Smoother

Her name is Lorna. Lorna Luft. That shouldn't—and won't—be difficult to remember. Yet she was once introduced, while singing in Atlantic City, as *Irna Lust*. Another emcee dubbed her *Laura Duft*. She is the second daughter of Judy Garland, the half-sister of Liza Minnelli, and the wife of musician Jake Hooker. She's sung all over the world, has a hit record in Germany, and is about to make her movie debut in *Grease 2*. It's a show-business history that only a vaudevillian could unravel—yet Lorna Luft is still in her 20's. Only her longevity makes her seem older.

"Nobody remembers that Lorna started at 17," recalled producer Allan Carr. It was Carr, with the late writer Bronte Woodard, who created for Luft the role of Paulette Rebchuck, the vamp of a pizza waitress in *Grease 2*. "The central thing about Lorna is this: She can be sexy, as in Olivia Newton-John, or funny, as in Eve Arden. Lorna can play both the star and the star's best friend."

These days Luft is playing her cards right. If the career started on a rocky road, it may be smoothing out. In Hollywood, she's up for two films and a TV pilot. In New York, two weeks ago, she celebrated her fifth wedding anniversary (to musician Hooker). "It was the 'Night of 100 Stars,'" Luft recalled the other afternoon in Malibu. "I called it the 'Night of 200,000 Limousines.' But I decided I was not going to spend my fifth anniversary at Radio City."

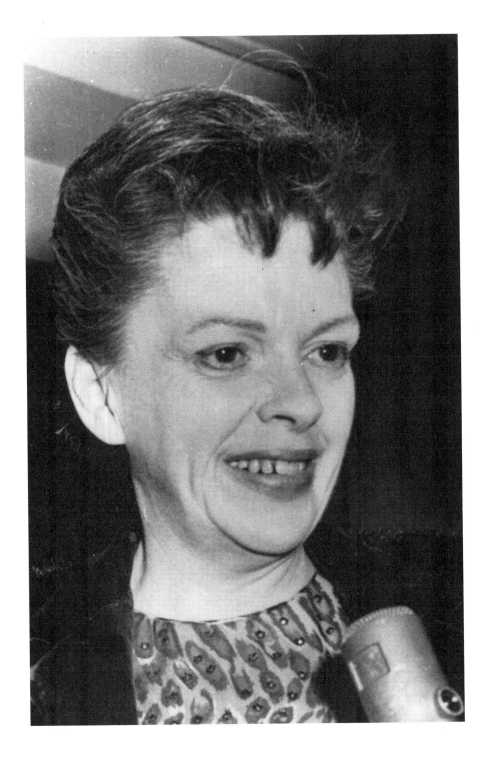

The attitude is just like Luft. A show-business baby, she's both like and unlike mother and sister. Lorna's just as funny, but more approachable. "I never had a chance to be a princess," she confided. And as a long beach afternoon unfolded, she explains why. It's a story for the show-biz history books.

Lorna, the first child by Garland and her third husband, Sid Luft, was named for Lorna Moon, a character in Clifford Odets' *Golden Boy.* She spent her infancy either in Holmby Hills, Beverly Hills or on the set of *A Star Is Born.* The Luft marriage was alternately stormy and sublime, though Lorna downplays the dark side. "The press would report that we children were kidnapped by Daddy," she remembers with a giggle. " 'Kidnapped' meant we were taken to Disneyland—so who minded? There was a *lot* of love."

When Lorna was 2, brother Joey was born: He became the apple of Judy's eye. "Yes, he was the prince. So I became the classic second child, fighting for love and survival." The siblings lived largely in a trunk, be it in London or Pocatello. Almost nothing about life was normal. "I remember seeing 'Leave It to Beaver' on TV for the first time," Luft recalls. "I thought it was so weird to see a family all live and eat together. I couldn't fathom it."

For years, there were those in show business who couldn't fathom Lorna Luft. "Do you want the obvious reasons—or the other reasons?" she asked openly.

"Well," she went on, "when your mother is a legend and your sister becomes *awfully* famous . . . then you're the *third.* You're an attraction, a curiosity."

Unlike mother and sister, she was both blonde and sexy. There were also some young, rowdy times. "But for years, I'd walk into a record company and they'd say, 'Why not do a disco version of "Over the Rainbow"?' And I'd say 'Oh, and is the flip side a rock version of "Cabaret"?' Then I'd leave the office."

What she never left, however, was the business of entertainment. At 16, Lorna was already playing the Palace with Judy. "Mama told me one thing. She said, 'You're not going to make it on my coattails.' She was right. Nobody is interested, once that door is opened. Everything Liza has she earned in spades. It's the hard way, and the only way. The door opens and also closes."

* * *

Luft learned it early: "I was in public high school in Los Angeles seeking just a little normalcy," she recalled, "and all of a sudden—whoosh—I'm going to Broadway. I was hired to play Lolita in an Alan Jay Lerner musical. So, two weeks before graduation, I left alone for New York, where I moved into the Barbizon Hotel for Women.

"I'm rehearsing 'Lolita' for a week and a half, and suddenly I am fired. Fired, in front of the whole company! Three years later I discover the director's wife thought the director had eyes for me."

Luft left Broadway for the Professional Children's School. (A classmate was Pia Zadora.) She also auditioned for everything from Off-Broadway's "Alice in Wonderland" to Broadway's "Sugar." "I got this call one day that David Merrick and Gower Champion wanted to see me for the lead in the musical of 'Some Like It Hot.' I knew I had to be too young. It was the Marilyn Monroe role. I was auditioned, then was stunned to be called back to read. Finally Gower Champion invited me to his house for lunch. 'I don't know how to tell you this,' he said. I answered, 'I *know*: I'm too young!' Was he relieved! I mean, I was in my *teens.*

"Next thing I know, David Merrick put me in 'Promises, Promises' on Broadway. Not too shabby, right? Michael Bennett choreographing, and so on. One day on the street I run into the producer who fired me from 'Lolita.' It was one of those moments. He said, 'What are you doing?' I told him I was doing real good. Here I was on Broadway, and 'Lolita' had already closed. It was karma."

The next experience was a nightmare. Managers, agents, advisers and others had decided Luft needed a career move—to saloons. They dictated she have Peter Matz arrangements, Halston gowns, chorus boys, the works. An act was devised. "They had me singing 'Am I Blue?,' torch songs, Billie Holiday songs. I said, 'I'm 18. How can I sing the blues when I'm not old enough to *have had* them yet?'"

She sang them anyway. Her debut engagement, at Atlantic City's now defunct Steel Pier, was legendary: "I'm driving in from Philly when I see these massive billboards reading 'JUDY GARLAND'S DAUGHTER! LIZA MINNELLI'S SISTER!' To see my name, you needed a magnifying glass. I still have the billboards.

"We're talking five shows a day, with a dressing room the size of a table. In it are the Halston gowns, the Matz arrangements, and half of the William Morris Agency. The club is by the ocean, so the waves are rolling in. My father says, 'What time do we dock?'"

The entourage didn't dock; it waited through the opening acts: "First, two acrobats with holes in their leotards. Then five chimpanzees wearing gold lame tuxedos and blonde wigs. The chimps had the dressing room next to mine. Then an adagio number where the dancer wore a chin strap to hold her wig on. She gets thrown around and lands on her ear lobes.

"Finally, my road manager walks in with a look of panic. They'd bused in 500 8-year-olds from a Philadelphia school—all patrol boys. And I'm supposed to sing the blues.

"So I get into the Halston gown; it's Labor Day, but freezing. It's my first time on a stage alone, and I'm introduced as *Irna Lust!* For the second show I'm introduced as *Laura Duft*. Not once did they get my name right."

In Europe, where she headed with a new act, they got it right. Luft changed her approach, aged-down the show and sold out arenas from Stockholm to Salzburg. She spent three years in London with her husband-to-be, who was enjoying his own career as a rock composer. (His tune "I Love Rock 'n' Roll" was Grammy-nominated this year.) "Finally you reach a point," admitted Luft, "when you have to come home. It meant starting all over again."

It meant, specifically, cattle-call auditions, episodic TV spots, and, finally, a long-run job. After playing "Grease" on Ohio's summer circuit, she got the lead in a touring company of "They're Playing our Song." It proved the best career move of all; the choreographer happened to be Pat Birch. A year later, Birch would direct *Grease 2.*

"Lorna had to be good onstage," explained Allan Carr. "Eight times a week in Akron or Hershey in a two-character show, you must deliver. It's optimum training. My first client, when I was a manager, was Marlo Thomas. It was very hard at first to get her work. She was simply the *daughter of*—. Until Jane Fonda broke the mold, there was that stigma. We put Marlo onstage in 'Sunday in New York,' and later in 'Barefoot in the Park,' and from there she could do anything. Lorna had been in on the end of the nightclub era. She was an opening act, and where would that lead? Liza had become a huge star, and impossible to follow. So Lorna went out and learned her trade."

She also got *Grease 2,* but not easily. First she went through another cattle call ("800 people, but I'm not a snob"). Then, a screen test, a watermelon diet that led to a 22-pound loss, a move to Los Angeles, a test for her first driver's license, and daily readings with proposed co-stars. Finally, she was the last star to be cast. "Everything I've ever gone through," Luft revealed, with a smile that lights up stages, "was worth it to hear Pat Birch say three words: 'You are Paulette.'

"I went into the bathroom at Paramount and cried so loud the crew thought I *lost* the part. I walked out of the bathroom and they were all standing there. Pat said, 'Meet Paulette.' They applauded. I cried for the next eight hours, including through dinner with my husband at Le Dome. The waiters thought he was divorcing me . . . It really is about paying dues. Pay them, and you win."

Luft, at that moment, turned her attention to the muzak blaring through the Malibu Cafe. "I always hear music in my head," she mused. It was a line Garland might have said—but the delivery was pure Lorna. Her mother may have been a legend and her sister awfully famous, but Lorna Luft—at that moment—was awfully happy.

Judy On Judy

"We were so elated and happy we didn't dream about asking just how much our salary was to be for the night. Mother again bought us new dresses. All our friends came. Dad sat in the first row. And we got a lot of applause. But when we opened our pay envelopes after the show we found fifty cents in each—and Mother had paid $10 each for our new dresses!"

—Judy Garland, quoted in an MGM press release, 1940

Credits

Kind permission has been granted to reprint the following:

"Let's Get Personal: Revealing Intimate and Intriguing Details About Judy Garland"
(From *Modern Screen,* October 1940.)

"Babes in the Woods" by Adela Rogers St. Johns
(From *The American Weekly,* supplement to the *Los Angeles Examiner,* March 18, 1951. Reprinted by permission of Hearst Corporation.)

"No More Tears for Judy" by Hedda Hopper
(From *Woman's Home Companion,* September 1954.)

"Judy Garland's Magic Word" by Liza Wilson
(From *The American Weekly,* supplement to the *Los Angeles Examiner,* September 26, 154. Reprinted by permission of Hearst Corporation.)

"The Rebirth of a Star" by Bosley Crowther
(From *The New York Times,* October 17, 1954. Copyright © 1954 by The New York Times Company. Reprinted by permission.)

"Folklore from Hollywood" by Naomi Wise
(From *San Francisco,* September 1983. Reprinted by kind permission of the author.)

"Judy Garland and Gay Men" by Richard Dyer
(Copyright © 1986 Richard Dyer. From *Heavenly Bodies: Film Stars and Society* by Richard Dyer. Reprinted with permission of St. Martin's Press, Incorporated. Reprinted with permission of Macmillan Press Ltd.)

"A Dialogue: Noel Coward and Judy Garland"
(From *Redbook,* November 1961. Coward material copyright © 1961. By permission of Michael Imison Playwrights Ltd., 28 Almeida St., London N1 1TD.)

"Crack-Up" by Joe Hyams
(From *Photoplay,* January 1957.)

"The TV Troubles of Judy Garland" by Richard Warren Lewis
(Reprinted from *The Saturday Evening Post,* December 7, 1963. © 1963.)

"Judy Garland: 'I've Been a Fool'" by Comer Clarke
(From *Titbits,* October 23, 1965.)

"The Plot against Judy Garland" by Judy Garland
(From *Ladies' Home Journal,* August 1967. © 1967, Meredith Corporation. All Rights Reserved. Used with the permission of *Ladies' Home Journal*® magazine.)

"Raised on Judy, or, What Chance Did a Boy Have?" by Rick McKay
(© 1996 by Rick McKay. Printed by kind permission of the author.)

"The Enigma of Judy Garland" by Ralph J. Gleason
(Reprinted by permission of the estate of Ralph J. Gleason and Jazz Casual Productions, Inc. All rights reserved. © Jazz Casual Productions, Inc.)

About the Editor

Author, journalist and television personality Ethlie Ann Vare has been writing and talking about history, pop culture, and the entertainment industry for more than a decade. She is best known as the "music gossip" on E! Entertainment Television's *The Gossip Show* and as a music critic for *The Hollywood Reporter*. Her work has been read in dozens of glossy publications, including *Billboard, Daily Variety,* and the award-winning *ROCK* magazine.

Throughout the '80s, Ethlie's syndicated newspaper column, "Rock On," was the #1 most read music feature in the United States and Canada. Today, her celebrity interviews and feature stories are published worldwide through Syndicated International Network. She also writes teleplays for action and mystery shows.

Vare's award-winning 1988 book *Mothers of Invention: From the Bra to the Bomb, Forgotten Women and their Unforgettable Ideas* is still used as a college and high school text.

Mothers of Invention spawned two texts about women: *Women Inventors and Their Discoveries* and *Adventurous Spirit: A Story About Ellen Swallow Richards.* It also won the American Library Association Award as one of the year's Best Books for Young Adults. Ethlie's most recent books are Boulevard's *Legend: Frank Sinatra and the American Dream* and *Diva: Barbra Streisand and the Making of a Superstar.*